TWO FACTOR THEORY OF CUSTOMER SERVICE

A COMPREHENSIVE, EASY TO READ GUIDE FOR INCREASING PROFITS

DAVID L. ELWOOD, Ph.D.

AuthorHouse™LLC
1663 Liberty Drive
Bloomington, IN 47403
www.authorhouse.com
Phone: 1-800-839-8640

Published by AuthorHouse 04/25/2014

ISBN: 978-1-4918-4442-7 (sc)
ISBN: 978-1-4918-4443-4 (e)

Library of Congress Control Number: 2013922693

This book is printed on acid-free paper.

DEDICATION

To my mother Mollie N. Elwood, sister Helen H. Haun, brothers Riley E. Burchfield and Raymond L. Elwood, and my mother-in-law Leona L. Jones who always extended acceptance, support, encouragement, and love to me for all worthy things I ever attempted to do; to my wife Ella M. Elwood whose support and love helped me finish this project; and, to six very special people who provide unending delight and inspiration every day of the week: Chase S. Elwood, Taylor B. Elwood, Jacob D. Elwood, Josie L. Elwood, Hudson A. Elwood, and Slader J. Elwood.

ACKNOWLEDGEMENTS

Thanks to the many people who influenced my ideas about customer service; these include our excellent staff members at Elwood Staffing who demonstrate day in and day out what it means to provide *Superior Customer Service*, the thousands of external customers who trust us to help them find competent dependable workers, the associates who accept assignments day by day and who show up day by day to do their jobs, and the many authors of customer service books who shared their experiences and insights about this greatly significant area of business activity.

Several people helped by showing interest, offering encouragement, or by reading earlier manuscripts and making suggestions for improvements. To them, I say a very special thank you for taking time from their busy schedules to assist me. They are Kimberly Randall, Amy Cone, Mandy Shell, Kristy Kramer, Len Nudi, Mark Niles, Stephanie Dwigans, Helen Hancock, Mark Shirai, Lorena Amaral, Clarence Webb, Judy Rodriguez, Alicia Hitchcock, Debbie Wolfe, Sarah Stair, Connie Whisner, Robin Gassaway, Wendy H. Elwood, Amber D. Elwood, Edie Garlock, Nancy Carey, David Carey, Addrea Brown, Theresa McCrady, Lia Elliott, Alan Balmer, Julie Sutton, Nick Seger, Jenna Hladik, Ella M. Elwood, William G. Elwood, Linda S. Elwood, Steve Hunnicutt, Mark S. Elwood, Steve Taylor, John A. Elwood, Penni Lashua, Mary Hughes Kendrick, and Michael D. Elwood. Lastly, my apology and my heartfelt thanks go to any other person who helped but was inadvertently left off this list.

PREFACE

The "*Two Factor Theory of Customer Service*" is a book rich with examples that highlight the significance of customer service and its impact on business success and profitability. This book is written by a successful business leader who was able to identify and define for the readership those elements that are critical to superior customer service. Dr. David L. Elwood has graciously shared with us how his company was able to transform the culture of Elwood Staffing to one that has unwavering commitment to providing superior customer service to all customers. Whatever your business or profession, you are likely to find something in the "*Two Factor Theory of Customer Service*" that will enhance your ability to deliver superior customer service to those whom you serve.

Marwan A. Wafa, Ph.D.
Vice Chancellor & Dean
Indiana University-Purdue University
Columbus

CONTENTS

INTRODUCTION

These introductory comments are intended to help readers anticipate the contents of the *Two Factor Theory of Customer Service,* to more fully understand the ideas presented, and to more completely assimilate those ideas into their views of customer service.

Purpose

The primary purpose of the *Two Factor Theory of Customer Service* is to increase business profits through improved understanding and practice of *Superior Customer Service.* A clear, consistent framework for approaching customer service issues is described. Some specific guidelines for providing *Superior Customer Service* concepts are discussed. Additionally, attempts are made to inspire readers to become passionate about customer service and to acquire new levels of awareness of the strong connections between positive customer service and high levels of profitability in all business enterprises.

The central theoretical idea presented is the *Two Factor Theory* of customer service. This theory states that each and every business transaction involves two factors, or two products. The first product, that is, the primary product, is the basis for any company to be in business. The *primary product* may be tangible or intangible. The second product in business transactions is the *customer service product.* The customer service product is almost always intangible. Whether or not it is thought about, talked about, planned for, or recognized, the customer service product is invariably present and goes hand in hand with the primary product.

Why should one write about the ***theory*** *of customer service rather than to catalog the many* ***techniques*** *that can be used to improve delivery of customer service?* The answer is that those having some grounding in theories of customer service are better prepared to think critically about customer service concepts and better equipped to put customer service ideas into practice than those who have not been exposed to theories.

One more comment is appropriate concerning theory versus technique. Most authors are pleased to have many people read their books—the more readers the better. Also, many (most?) authors are biased concerning how important their ideas are and how much better off certain people or certain sub-groups in society would be if "*only they knew*" about the ideas that authors are so eager to share with them. Author Dave Elwood would like for many people to read the *Two Factor Theory of Customer Service*—in that respect he is like most other authors, but in fairness to those readers who may pick up the *Two Factory Theory of Customer Service* expecting a book filled to the brim with specific techniques, strategies, guidelines, and suggestions for coping with day by day customer service challenges, the *Two Factor Theory of Customer Service* is probably not the answer. The *Two Factor Theory ...* focuses mainly upon theory, framework, definitions, and customer service as a professional discipline, rather than upon the abundant specific techniques that are helpful in the daily delivery of *Superior Customer Service*. Undoubtedly, this frank recognition of the central focus of the *Two Factor Theory ...* will result in the loss of some readers. Author Dave Elwood hopes the loss will be small.

Customer Service: A Professional Discipline

Many people interested in the customer service field see it as a professional activity. If the field of customer service is indeed a professional activity, then it makes sense for one to approach customer service as a discipline the same as attorneys, physicians, and scientists approach their fields as disciplines.

Aspiring attorneys do not immediately plunge into the practice of law; those interested in medicine do not just *hang up a shingle*; and those interested in science do not simply declare themselves to be scientists and start producing significant new findings. Typically, what one does is study theories of law, medicine, or science in the classroom, receive supervised practical experience in one's specialty, and then, after passing appropriate examinations, begin professional practice of one's specialty.

These examples about law, medicine, and science were presented to make this point: *Should not those who profess serious professional interest in customer service work hard to develop coherent, valid theories in this area and should not those entering this field of study and service expect to be exposed to such theories?* The answer is "*Yes.*"

Intended Audiences

The *Two Factor Theory of Customer Service* is intended mainly for three groups of people, but its concepts have application to all people in all types of businesses.

Group One is made up of individual providers within a company or sole proprietors who want to do better jobs of serving the customer and who are searching for more effective and helpful ways to look at and to think about customer service. Some readers may immediately conclude: *Well, I guess this book is not for me since I'm not a customer service provider.* Here is a suggestion for those readers: *Stick with the*

***Two Factor Theory of Customer Service** from beginning to end and you will see that you are much more of a customer service provider than you ever imagined.* At the least, reading the *Two Factor Theory of Customer Service* will lead to improvement in one's ability to discern when he is and when he is not receiving good customer service.

Group Two members are mid-level managers who want to inspire higher levels of customer service performance among their front line co-workers, but have failed to do so because they have not had a clear picture of the customer service field. The *Two Factor Theory of Customer Service* can add clarity to their perceptions of customer service and assist them in showing the decisiveness, energy, and enthusiasm necessary to lead co-workers to higher levels of customer service delivery.

Group Three is comprised of senior managers such as owners, presidents, CEO's, and other executive staff who would like to elevate their entire organizations to higher levels of customer service performance, but, similar to mid-level managers, have failed to act because they have not found acceptable frameworks for looking at customer service issues. Because their own perceptions have not been clear and compelling, they have not felt justified in projecting a customer service vision or in demanding the top-to-bottom commitment of time, energy, and money that would be required to lead entire companies to higher levels of customer service performance. *The Two Factor Theory of Customer Service* can be the foundation for a vision and for the deep commitment needed to move entire companies to higher levels of performance.

Industry Focus

The business background of the *Two Factor Theory of Customer Service* author Dave Elwood consists of having had an office for the practice of clinical psychology, having used pre-employment tests to help select business personnel for hiring and promotion, and having worked in the temporary staffing industry. Concepts presented in the *Two Factor Theory of Customer Service* are clearly applicable to the staffing and talent acquisition industries; however, attempts have been made to explain these concepts in very general terms; the reason has been to make it easy for them to be applied to other businesses and professions.

The ideas in the *Two Factor Theory of Customer Service* apply to settings as diverse as retail stores, food vendors at sporting events, newspaper delivery services, banking, catalog sales, real estate sales, transportation services, manufacturing, governmental services, and professional practices such as law, accounting, dentistry, and medicine. Actually, these ideas are applicable to any person in any type of business.

Rise of Elwood Staffing

Concepts presented in the *Two Factor Theory of Customer Service* are intimately connected to the rise of Elwood Staffing. In a nutshell, here is the Elwood Staffing story. In 1980, author Dave Elwood opened an office for private clinical psychological practice. Also, psychological testing expertise was offered to help with pre-employment personnel selection problems in business and industry.

In 1995, the pre-employment testing business started evolving into a temporary staffing service. The demand for temporary staffing rose like a tidal wave. Almost all time and energy in the office were redirected toward handling the on-rush of staffing demands. *Elwood Consulting Services*, the name of the pre-employment side of the business, was changed to *Elwood Staffing Services, Inc.* to better reflect the main work activity within the office.

In 1995, there was one office and a staff of three fulltime people plus one half-time person. Twelve years later in 2007, the business had grown to 38 offices in seven states with an average weekly payroll of approximately 6,500 temporary workers, and annual revenue of $160 million.

In the fall of 2013, six years later, Elwood Staffing had grown to about 190 offices, did business in 31 states and Canada, had average weekly payroll of around 28,000 temporary workers, and annual revenue for 2013 was projected to be $800 million. Most of the author's ideas about customer service evolved from within his experiences at Elwood Staffing.

Approaches to Customer Service

It was estimated in year 2000 that more than 600 books had been published on customer service topics. If one allows for additional books published since 2000 and broadens the focus to include books that do not cite the word *customer* in their titles or subtitles, but still give major emphasis to this topic, then the number of books published on customer service could well reach into the thousands.

Customer service literature reflects a huge variety of emphases, interpretations, and perspectives that can be used to try to understand customer service experiences. Because of these many different approaches, it is fully understandable why some people interested in customer service could ask questions such as these: *What is most important? Is anything really essential? Is customer service really anything more than a never ending series of positive, unique, and totally anecdotal customer experiences that defy analysis? Where do I start to acquire the best basic understanding of customer service?*

To answer questions such as these, it may be helpful to have some general categories for classifying customer service literature: 1) *anecdotal accounts*—examples of brilliant one-of-a-kind experiences of superior customer service, 2) *case studies*—detailed accounts showing how certain admirable patterns of customer service evolved, 3) *company stories*—A to Z explanations of how positive, companywide programs of customer service developed, 4) *how-to guides*—outlining of both attitudes and actions that lead to good customer service, 5) *research reviews*—compilations of objective reports, or scientific studies of the effectiveness of certain customer service practices, 6) *training manuals*—formal programs that train participants to become competent in specific aspects of good customer service, and 7) *systematic frameworks*—approaches that attempt to develop broad frameworks of understanding within which to fit the huge variety of customer service experiences.

These categories are neither pure nor exclusionary. Also, most books on customer service include a measure of inspiration or exhortation about the value of customer service. A given book may include only one or several categories of information. Depending upon one's interests and motivation, books in each category may be helpful.

A Systematic Framework

The *Two Factor Theory of Customer Service* is best classified as a *systematic framework*. A theory about how to look at and how to understand customer service is presented, and clear definitions are offered for concepts that are central to understanding customer service processes. A basic idea in the *Two Factor Theory of Customer Service* is that customer service is best understood as comprised of *customer service events* and that these ***events*** may be thought of as having a limited number of characteristics or dimensions that help describe them.

Attempts are made to create passion for the customer service perspective and practical suggestions are made for delivering customer service products. Customer service events and processes are viewed from comprehensive perspectives so that proposed insights may have wide applications. No idea or theory works flawlessly when applied to the real world. Nevertheless, it is important to work toward coherent sets of ideas when referring to significant aspects of business experiences whether they are called customer service or anything else.

Practicality of Theories

Some business people shy away from the word theory. When they think of theories, they think of academia and people living in *ivory towers.* They may hold attitudes that go something like this:

Look, I am required on a daily basis to cope with extremely demanding practical problems. I don't have time to read about theories. The assistance I need is for clear-cut suggestions and guidelines that can help me know what to do right now.

Attitudes such as these are easy to understand. It is often true that people whose main interests lie in the creation and assessment of theories spend so much time weighing highly abstract implications of different theories that they never get around to making suggestions for how to handle practical problems. Regarding the *Two Factor Theory of Customer Service*, it can be adopted *right now* as a starting point and method for trying to understand customer service processes. The theory is clear and compelling; by adopting this theory, one will have engaged a powerful technique that can help generate problem solutions.

More than a half century ago, the well known psychologist Kurt Lewin (1945) said "*there is nothing more practical than a good theory.*" That thought applies well to the *Two Factor Theory of Customer Service.*

The main concept of the *Two Factor Theory* … is not based upon a history of well-controlled scientific studies, but such candor should stop no one from adopting and using the *Two Factor Theory* … It can shine a bright light on the pathway leading to *Superior Customer Service.* As better, more productive theories are proposed, they will be adopted throughout the customer service discipline.

CHAPTER 1

THE TWO FACTOR THEORY OF CUSTOMER SERVICE

The *Two Factor Theory of Customer Service* provides backdrop for everything said in this book. Therefore, it is introduced first so that readers may have a head start for understanding how author Dave Elwood looks at and presents other customer service issues.

The *Two Factor Theory of Customer Service* states that each and every business enterprise provides a minimum of two products. ***First*** is the *main product* or range of products that may vary all the way from things tangible and concrete such as *lawn mowers* to things intangible and abstract such as *legal advice.* Main products are deliverable; they go directly to the customer. ***Second*** is the *customer service product* that is almost entirely intangible and abstract. Furthermore, the *Two Factor Theory* ... states that a *customer service event* occurs each time a customer exchanges money for main products and recurs each time thereafter when there is customer-provider contact to address any issue about the main product or about the customer service product whether or not additional money is exchanged. Customer service happens, good or bad, whether or not one is aware of it.

The meaning of the *Two Factor Theory* ... can be seen in this example: A woman entered a bookstore, browsed through some titles, selected one book for purchase, walked to a checkout counter, and handed her book to a clerk who rang-up the sale. She paid cash for the book and left the store. Upon arriving at home, she discovered that a manufacturing error resulted in smudging making several pages of the book unreadable. She took the book back to the store and made an even exchange of a defective book for a non-defective book.

In this example, there was initial contact with exchange of money for a book and later contact to return a book during which time no money changed hands. The *Two Factor Theory .....* states that customer service was provided during both visits. Customer service consisted of the entire range of all interactions, both subtle and obvious, that occurred between the customer and the clerk from the moment of the sale to the conclusion of the second visit.

If one accepts the basic notion of the ***Two Factor Theory of Customer Service****, what are the implications? What are some of the pathways down which this theory would lead us?*

Continuous Presence of Customer Service

The most obvious implication of the *Two Factor Theory ...* is that whenever products of any kind are sold, customer service is *always* present. It is never optional. It is always there. It is not one of those *take-it- or- leave- it* types of things where, if one wants it, he embraces it, and if he doesn't want it, he walks away from it. The *Two Factor Theory ...* implies that neither executives, managers, supervisors, nor any other person or group of people can avoid customer service. It will not go away. It can be denied, ignored, neglected, discounted, and discouraged, but it hangs around anyway. And, not only does it hang around, it continues to have unrelenting impact on sales, repeat business, profitability, loyalty, and morale. Customer service does not need to be recognized to have impact. If leaders, directors, frontline staff, or anyone else acts as if customer service has neither existence nor importance, it is not deterred; it continues to affect and to drive emotions and behavior in the customer.

Each time a business transaction takes place, customer service occurs. It may occur as a delightful experience that leaves the customer feeling good, or it may occur as an unexpectedly negative experience that spoils the rest of the customer's day. Taking the time and effort to deliver excellent customer service may be seen as a nuisance to some business people who see it as interfering with their ability to increase sales and profits. But, to most business people, customer service is seen as a golden opportunity to out maneuver, out run, out serve, and outperform the competition. A company may do away with an area in a store called the **Customer Service Department**, but it cannot do away with customer service. A company may ignore important customer service issues, but it cannot excuse itself from the impact of poor customer service events.

Main Product Improvement

Author Dave Elwood recalls, as a teenager living in New Castle, Indiana, hearing about a wealthy farmer who, in the early days of the automobile era, drove a new car and was so impressed by everything about the car that he felt it would be impossible for such a car to ever be improved upon; his response was to buy two of these cars, one to drive and the other to keep in his garage until he needed it.

Things have changed dramatically since the early era of the automobile. Now, everyone expects change, quite rapid change in most areas of life, especially in consumer technology goods, and many want to be among the first to buy and to try out the latest models and styles that become available. Main products have always changed, but the rates of change are much more rapid now than in the past.

Customer Service Product Improvement

If primary products are improving at a rapid pace and if, as the *Two Factor Theory of Customer Service* argues, primary products and customer service products are tied closely together, what is the implication of primary product improvement for customer service product improvement? The implication is clear: customer service products should change, advance, and improve along with associated improvements in primary products.

Consider this scenario: A bright, charming mobile phone salesperson was highly successful. She loved her work, loved helping customers, and delighted all customers and potential customers who came into contact with her. In a nutshell, she gave *Superior Customer Service.* However, there was a problem. She decided against participating in additional training, instruction, reading, or study that would qualify her to discuss advanced features that were present in all new model mobile phones. The end result was inevitable: some of her customer service tools would become outdated; there would be questions she could not answer and problems she could not solve. Her ability to deliver *Superior Customer Service* would gradually erode. Because she was bright and charming, she would continue to make sales. But, she would be less effective than other equally bright and charming sales people who had acquired necessary new customer service skills. The salesperson that increased and improved her customer service skills would sell more higher-priced phones, would make higher commissions, and would earn greater profits for her employer. *The customer service product needs to improve step by step with the main product: that is the implication of the Two Factor Theory of Customer Service.*

Continuous Assessment of Products

The main products of any company are usually assessed on a continuous basis to make sure they meet certain quality standards.

Such assessments are not performed on a casual, do-it-if-you-feel-like-it basis. Absolutely not! If one were making precision items such as ball bearings, tolerances would be expressed in thousandths of an inch or ten thousandths of an inch. One might gather samples of manufactured items and perform tests on them *many times during an eight hour shift*. If one's main products were canned food items, the manufacturing standard would be for them to be free of foreign objects, impurities, contaminants, and organisms that could cause the food to spoil or cause consumers to become ill. One would very likely perform *ongoing tests and assessments* to make sure all food products met required quality standards.

If one's main products were pharmaceuticals, highly detailed standards would be established for selecting ingredients, eliminating impurities, eliminating harmful bacteria, and guaranteeing that all manufactured products, when used properly, would perform according to expectancies. One would develop highly specific systems for *assessing each and every step, turn, stage, and phase* in the processes of manufacturing, transporting, delivering, storing, and using of his or her product.

What do assessments of ball bearings, food items, and pharmaceuticals have to do with the Two Factor Theory of Customer Service? Here is the point: If the *Two Factor Theory ...* is true and if tangible main products such as ball bearings, food items, and pharmaceuticals are subject to thorough, on-going assessments to help assure that they meet high quality standards, then does it not make sense that *customer service products* associated with these main products should also be subject to continuous assessments to assure that they as well shall meet high quality standards? If a poor quality main product could result in decreasing sales and profits, is it not also possible that a poor quality customer service product could result in decreasing sales and profits?

The *Two Factor Theory*... implies that customer service products should receive the same ongoing rigorous assessments and measurements as do main products. *The measurement techniques used for a main tangible product such as ball bearings (e.g., micrometers) will, of course, be different from the measurement techniques used for the often intangible and abstract product of customer service (e.g., customer rating scale from 1 to 10), but many of the basic statistical techniques used to analyze these two types of data are the same.* Furthermore, one can be just as confident that scientific assessments of customer service products using rating scales will provide helpful information as he can be confident that scientific assessments of ball bearings using micrometers will provide helpful information. In the case of customer service, the results will tell if the service is good or bad as compared to some standard; in the case of ball bearings, the results will tell whether the ball bearings are too little, too big, or just right as compared to a design specification. The essential point is that trustworthy analyses can be performed on both tangible main products and intangible, but highly related, customer service products.

The current state of affairs is that many business leaders are quite relaxed about the need to continuously assess their customer service products. They are not hostile toward the idea of customer service assessment; they simply see little need for it. But, what if a convenient, accurate, and easy to use system for assessing the quality of customer service were installed in a business, and if, furthermore, the system would reveal that customer service quality was poor and getting worse? Most business owners and managers would *perk-up* and would recognize that poor customer service could be the answer to decreasing sales and/or profits and that something should be done about the problem, or they would recognize that failures in the customer service arena were causing profits and sales to be lower than what they could be if only customer service were better. The concept of *quality control* applies to both the *main product* and to the *customer service product.*

Cost of Customer Service

What about the cost of customer service? If customer service is a product that goes hand in hand with the main products of a company, then most serious business leaders will ask about the cost of customer service. Can we afford it? What will be the initial outlay in order to get a customer service program up and running? Is there an economy grade customer service program? What will be the monthly cost to maintain a respectable customer service product? If we look at customer service from an ROI (return on investment) perspective, will it pay off?

These are legitimate questions that should be asked about any business activity or business investment. Fortunately, the answers to these questions are positive and may be surprising. To begin, one does not have to worry about whether or not a business can afford a customer service program. The fact is that each business is already paying for a customer service program and has been doing so for as long as it has been in business. Furthermore, there is no need to be concerned about getting a customer service program up and running. It's already up and running. It may not be a very good program, but it's there and has been there all along. Regarding the possibility of installing an economy grade program, if one has not been paying attention to customer service issues, then, that's probably what he has been paying for all along and that is probably what is in place at this very moment.

The largest expense one will incur in upgrading a customer service program will be the money spent to upgrade his or her own attitudes and to train his or her staff to adopt new ways of looking at and serving customers. One will not need to worry about buying a lot of new equipment—customer service is mostly a human, interpersonal process. Sometimes technology can help, but it's not the main component. One may have to change some personnel, especially if he has employees who maintain essentially anti-customer attitudes and resist all suggestions that they should make fundamental changes in how they see customers. Again, establishing a program for *Superior Customer Service* is more a matter of awareness, attitude, style, personal touch, caring, training, and commitment than it is about expensive equipment and big budgets.

One's monthly budget for customer service consists of the costs that have been occurring regularly all along. One's budget will not change if all he or she wants to do is to stick with the *economy grade* program that is now in place. If one wants to upgrade his or her customer service program, money will have to be spent, but simply getting the change process underway need not be overly expensive. One can ascend a mountain in a slow steady pace.

Upgrading a customer service program will cost more in early stages than after the program has reached a level of maturity. A useful analogy can be drawn between customer service and the manufacturing of a new part. Most of the costs for manufacturing a new part come in the early stages of the process. These include visualizing the part, preparing blueprints for the part, building the tools needed to make the part, and finally starting production. Once mass production is underway, the cost per manufactured part drops dramatically and the *yield* rises significantly.

The same thing is true for customer service. Once all of the elements of a *Superior Customer Service* program have been conceived, designed, put into place, and the whole company has risen to a higher level of performance, it will be less expensive to stay on top than it was to get on top. Each person in the company will be a day-by-day, constant reminder to every other person in the company that

Superior Customer Service to individual customers and establishing and sustaining a *Superior Customer Service* culture are goals that are shared in common by everyone in the company.

Enhanced Status of Customer Service as a Product

Another implication of the *Two Factor Theory* ... is that calling *customer service* a *product* will enhance its status as a business event that deserves attention, study, and priority. When one thinks of products, items coming to mind are things that can be looked at, touched, measured, weighed, and counted. One thinks of products as substantial, physical, and objective. People hold such biases even though they are aware that intangible and abstract things such as psychotherapy, legal advice, and financial services are often referred to as *products.*

When customer service is looked at as *simply a service* as opposed to being a product and when it is seen as merely optional as opposed to being an integral part of business transactions, one may be tempted to adopt an attitude such as this:

Customer service is usually a good thing if one has the right kinds of people to provide it and it's probably not going to hurt anything, but we don't have to worry too much about it. Our products are so good that they sell themselves. We'll get along OK.

On the other hand, those who look at customer service as a *real product* that is a built-in, integral aspect of business transactions will take it much more seriously than those who see it as "only a service." Business leaders will be more determined to know something about it, to train for it, to measure it, and to monitor it in the same way as main products are monitored. The ever present, unavoidable, and irrepressible customer service product should be embraced by everyone who truly seeks the highest level of business success.

CHAPTER 2

DEFINITIONS OF CUSTOMERS

Some people ascribe a single meaning to the word customer: *a customer is a person who buys things.* In contrast, those who have studied the word and have deep interest in customer service issues see additional ways of defining the term. *Two Factor Theory of Customer Service* author Dave Elwood believes that awareness of the full range of customer definitions and their appropriate uses can increase one's chances of delivering *Superior Customer Service.* In this chapter, some well established customer terms such as *internal* and *external customers* are reviewed and some new terms, namely *primary customer* and *secondary customer,* are presented and defined. Text Box 2-1 provides a summary of customer definitions.

Personhood of the Customer

One of the most fundamental facts about the concept of customer is that *it is best perceived as referring to a person, an individual.* In general, customers are not departments, divisions, offices, shops, plants, factories, mills, companies, corporations, associations, institutions, organizations, or branches of government. Customers exist within these organizations, but organizations per se are not usually thought of as customers. This concept is important to keep in mind as one tries to establish accounts and tries to provide *Superior Customer Service* to those accounts.

Types of Customers	**Customer Definitions**
Traditional	*Outside customers who buy things*
Primary	*Outside customers who buy things*
External	*Outside customers who buy things*
Internal	*Colleagues in one's own company (buyer or provider)*
Secondary (1)	*All in-house colleagues in provider company*
Secondary (2)	*In-house colleagues of primary customers who have influenced buying decisions and are known to a provider*
Secondary (3)	*Job applicants (associates) who work for staffing companies*
Corporate	*Corporations (companies)that acquire customer status as legal entities*
Prospective	*Anyone that a person believes could become a buyer*
Potential	*Anyone that a person believes could become a buyer*

Text Box 2-1

Traditional Definition of Customer

A customer is a person who buys things. This basic definition fits the majority of buying activities in all settings. But, sometimes it is difficult to identify the customer. For example, a person thinking seriously about how to define the word customer cannot go far before concluding that terms such as *prospective customer* or *potential customer* are required to help maintain clear distinctions between people who have *actually bought something* versus people who *may buy something*. Customers have bought something; customers may give repeat business; *prospective customers* have bought nothing and may never buy something.

Customers and prospective customers are two dramatically different groups. If, as Cooper (2010) suggested, *The Customer Signs Your Paycheck*, what does the prospective customer sign? He signs nothing. Customers are scarce compared to prospective customers. Prospective customers may number in the hundreds, thousands, or millions. Real customers can sometimes be counted on one's fingers and toes. Most salespeople know that real customers are hard to find. Customers make it possible for one to stay in business, and it is delivery of excellent customer service that helps retain existing customers. Prospective customers give one a reason to keep on trying; they give hope; they motivate salespeople to try to transform prospective customers into real customers. While one should discern clearly in his or her mind the customer-prospect divide, prospective customers should always be shown the greatest sensitivity and respect that is possible.

The sharp distinction drawn between *customers* and *prospective customers* could imply that prospective customers are unimportant. In truth, *prospective customers* are greatly important. At the start of any business, there are no customers. If one did not have at least *prospective customers*, there would be no possibility of succeeding in business. What is singularly advocated here is that providers maintain crystal clear perceptions as to who is and who is not a customer. At the end of the day, it is the customer who makes it possible for one to stay in business.

The traditional definition of the word customer is clearly illustrated in retail settings. For example, the simple word *customer* may be fully adequate for describing a person entering an ice cream store, making a purchase, and leaving the store—a process that may take three minutes or less. One knows who the customer is and one knows who the provider is. But, things are not always so simple.

As items being sold increase in price from less than a dollar to millions of dollars, as sales cycles increase from one or two minutes to days, weeks, months, and even years, and as transaction complexities increase from one customer and one provider to teams of people on the customer side negotiating with teams of people on the provider side, then the question of who the customer is and is not and the type of customer with which one may be dealing become important. There are other complications as well. Interactions become strung out over time. A few minutes are required to complete a transaction when one buys an ice cream cone, but properly and continuously serving a multi-million dollar account may take months and years. To deal with the complex array of provider-customer interactions that are a part of business-to-business relationships, one needs a well-developed nomenclature to identify customers, to describe their roles, and to understand how to manage customer-provider interactions.

Companies as Customers

If customers are individual people, why is it so commonplace to hear people refer to companies, especially large well-known companies, as customers? Mostly, it should be the exception rather than the rule to refer to companies and other organizational entities as customers, but there are valid reasons for doing so.

First, it is fitting to name a company as a customer if naming individuals as customers would seem odd or cryptic. For example, if a salesperson were talking to a potential customer and were to say "*I'm pleased to say we do business with Tom Johnson and Jane Green,*" the potential customer could feel such an answer was strange or odd. On the other hand if the salesperson should say, "*We do business with Coca-Cola, and IBM is a customer of ours,*" useful information would be conveyed, and one would project the idea that his or her company was sufficiently well-established, respected, and successful that it had formed business relationships with Fortune 100 companies.

Second, there are times when corporations, or companies, acquire *customer status* as legal entities. Corporations or companies may bear certain contractual-legal liabilities and responsibilities that would never be assigned to individuals within those companies. In such cases, companies, not individuals, are rightly identified as customers.

Third, companies provide organizational frameworks that often perpetuate business agreements with provider companies long after the individuals who negotiated such agreements have left these companies. In such cases, it would make sense and be perfectly reasonable to refer to a company as a *customer* and it would make little sense to insist on referring to a departed employee as the customer.

Despite legitimate reasons for seeing companies as customers, one should mostly focus upon individuals as customers, not upon organizations and legal entities. When things go well with an account, it is usually because a provider has worked hard to please one or more individual customers within that company, not because the provider has influenced *whole departments, divisions, or entire companies* to approve of the product or service made available by the provider.

External and Internal Customers

Many authors feel it makes sense to divide customers into two types, *external* and *internal* (e.g., Albrecht, 1994; Kaufman, 2012; Whiteley, 1991). *External customers* are defined as the people who buy things from us, a quite traditional and standard way of thinking about the word customer. *Internal customers* are defined as one's fellow staff members and colleagues who all work in the same company.

The rationale for calling one's colleagues *internal customers* is often un-explained, but it appears to be related to the idea that if it is a good thing to give special attention and treatment to the outside people called *external customers,* why would it not be a good thing to give the same special attention and treatment to one's in-house colleagues and to refer to them as *internal customers?* Be respectful to the external prospective customer and one may get a sale—one may convert a *prospect* into a *real customer.* Continue to be respectful to the customer and one may get another sale. In the same fashion, be respectful to fellow employees (i.e., *internal customers*), and they may help one's efforts to acquire and to retain *external customers.*

If a salesperson has a strained relationship with an in-house colleague (somehow the colleague has been offended), this state of affairs could work against the salesperson getting a sale as much as for an external prospective customer to say "*No*" to a sales presentation. It would be unnecessary for the offended colleague to take any overtly negative action against the salesperson. Should a colleague feel uncomfortable around a salesperson, that colleague could potentially hurt the salesperson by simply neglecting to go slightly out of his or her own way to take some optional action that could greatly help a salesperson to get a sale or retain a customer.

Therefore, if in-house colleagues can influence getting business and keeping business, why not call both the "internal colleague" and the "outside-contact" customers, *internal customers* and ex*ternal* *customers*? Why not try to serve both the *internal* and *external customers* equally well? The better one serves the *internal customer*, the more motivated that person will be to give *Superior Customer Service* to the provider and to the *external customer*.

In summary, if it's wise to give good treatment to *external customers* because they give us sales that keep us in business, then it should also be wise to give good treatment to *internal customers* because they too can help us get business and retain business.

Internal Customer Concept Questioned

Not everyone thinks the practice of referring to one's colleagues as internal customers is a good idea. Bell & Bell (2003) asserted that colleagues were quite different from customers and that referring to them as internal customers was a "*flawed concept*." They argued it would be better simply to refer to colleagues as "*partners*," not customers. They objected to the term internal customer on two grounds: 1) "*... it creates a power struggle over who thinks who is in charge, and* 2) *it diverts "... the attention of both parties on(to) internal conflict rather than on(to) the real customer—the one writing the checks*."

At Elwood Staffing, there is no evidence that referring to one's colleagues as customers has been problematic. Colleagues have been referred to as customers for many years. The practice has been taken in stride by everyone. Whenever the concept arises during in-house discussions, the implicit reaction of everyone has been that each person doing his or her job well helps everyone within the company and increases the chances that great customer service will be given to external customers. Furthermore, use of the terms *external customer* and *internal customer* appears to be a widely accepted practice (e.g., Zeithaml, Parasuraman, & Berry, 1990; Willingham, 1992;

Whiteley & Hessan, 1996; Massnick, 1997; Snow & Yanovitch, 2003; Schmitt, 2003; Lawfer, 2004; Blackshaw, 2008; Bailey & Leland, 2008; Goodman, 2009; Hyken, 2009; Kaufman, 2012).

The more broadly one defines the word customer, the more one assures that no potential customers or prospective customers will be overlooked. However, it is possible to focus one's efforts too widely and thereby lose sight of the very people who would be most likely to become real customers. Someone quipped that a salesperson who was not doing very well did not know the difference between a *prospect* and a *suspect*. A prospect is someone who has the authority to buy, the means to buy, and who may buy. In marked contrast, a *suspect* is someone who for any number of reasons is highly unlikely ever to buy.

If one is in sales and cannot distinguish clearly between a *customer*, a *prospective customer*, and a *suspect*, precious time (which equals money) will be wasted talking to the wrong people. The sales person will *spin his wheels* or *bark up the wrong tree*. And, what will happen? He will fail to win business and to create value for his employer. Eventually, he will be released or will quit due to frustration and lack of results. What is true for salespeople is also true for customer service providers. One needs to be so courteous, polite, respectful, and helpful to all people who come into one's business environment that outside observers would be unable to detect differences in how people are treated, but providers need, in their own minds, to discern clearly between *customers* and *prospective customers*.

Primary and Secondary Customers

The terms *primary customer* and *secondary customer* are introduced to recognize that customer buying decisions may be influenced by people other than the one identified person making the final decision to buy or not to buy. The term *primary customer* refers to the standard, traditional definition of customer—*a person who buys things.* The term *secondary customer* is introduced to recognize and to emphasize the fact that *co-workers* of the *primary customer* may influence the final buying decision of the *primary customer.*

Primary customers are special people because their buying habits keep one in business. Without these traditional, external customers, one does not have a business. One may have a wonderful product and a brilliant, delightful, dedicated group of salespeople and other employees, but if customer interest and demand are not present, and customers do not submit orders for one's products, the business will fail and everyone will be out looking for other jobs.

Three specific groups of people are called *secondary customers. The* ***first group*** *of secondary customers comes from the co-worker ranks of primary customers.* If a provider is aware that a co-worker of the *primary customer* has influenced the buying behavior of the *primary customer*, then, that person becomes a *secondary customer* to the provider. However, simply knowing the identity of a secondary customer is not necessarily helpful information. For any number of reasons related to practical opportunities or protocol, a provider may never have contact with or may never influence a secondary customer. But, a provider's awareness of the *secondary customer* label gives him or her potential advantage over other providers that do not possess this conceptual tool.

The ***second group*** *of secondary customers is defined as internal staff members of the provider's company.* The rationale for seeing one's own internal staff members as secondary customers is that they have such abundant opportunities to influence the course of business with *external customers*, or *primary customers.* How they perform their jobs impacts the *main products* and *customer service products* that are delivered to primary customers. The influence of one's internal staff members is usually indirect, but it is continuous and pervasive. *All internal staff members of a provider company are by definition secondary customers.* When these in-house *secondary customers* are focused, effective, and thoroughly dedicated to providing good customer service, things will bode well for everyone.

One could say the same things about flight crews and flight attendants on passenger airplanes as have been said about staffing company internal employees. Flight crews and flight attendants do not buy tickets, but they have a lot to do with whether or not passengers will be happy and will buy more tickets from the same airline in the future. To the executive leadership of a passenger airline company, the business traveler who buys a ticket is a *primary customer*, but some equally important customers are the *secondary customers* consisting of flight crews and flight attendants that help determine whether or not *primary customers* will purchase more tickets. Indeed, to the executive leadership of an airline, flight crews and attendants are *secondary customers.*

The ***third group*** *of secondary customers is somewhat unique to the staffing industry; this group is comprised of temporary workers, often called associates, who have been assigned to perform jobs for external customers.* All people working in the staffing industry see associates as important, but most do not see them as a type of customer. Associates have no influence at all on whether or not a staffing company is able to win an order to supply 20 people to perform a special two week job for the owner of a warehouse. However, whether or not the workers sent by the staffing company are able to perform the work correctly, take instructions well, show up on time, never miss work, and are felt to be all around good employees will have an enormous bearing on whether or not the owner of the warehouse orders more workers from this same staffing company. It is clear why *associates* constitute a class of *secondary customers.* How associates perform on the job dramatically affects how successful staffing companies will be at keeping business and growing business with the same customer.

Most people are aware that co-workers, associates, friends, relatives, and even strangers may significantly impact decision making processes of *external customers.* But, heretofore, there has been no commonly accepted label or name to use to identify these people. The *Two Factor Theory of Customer Service* author, Dave Elwood, is unaware of any attempt in customer service literature to give a label to or to identify the group of people that are herein named *secondary customers.* By calling a group of people a special type or special class of customer, namely *secondary customers*, they become easier to identify, are brought into one's awareness, and chances are increased that one may have a positive impact on them, and, indirectly, may enjoy increased influence on the primary customer. People are abundant. Prospective customers are less abundant. Real *customers*, people who have made and continue to make purchases are the rarest of all. One needs to do all he can to legitimately enhance his ability to influence customers.

Value of Different Customer Definitions

The practical value of having different definitions for customers is that it helps one think more clearly about customers and all other people and enables one to behave more precisely and effectively toward customers. The informed provider understands that most of the time *prospects* are more important than *suspects*, that *customers* are more important than *non-customers*, that *external customers* are more important than *internal customers*, and that *primary customers* are more important than *secondary customers.*

However, at the same time, no matter how a person may be perceived or labeled, people do not want to be taken for granted or to be treated with implied disrespect. If a person is a *prospective customer*, he or she does not want providers or salespeople acting as though his or her *right to choose, elect, select,* or *decide* does not exist, or has been taken away. When people are treated in such ways they often feel demeaned—many will drift toward other providers who are willing to give them *respect.* It is with these new providers that *demeaned prospects* place orders and, thereby, become *real customers.* As a concluding thought, one should treat even the so-called *suspect* respectfully. The reason is that *suspects* sometimes become *prospects* and *prospects* often become *customers.*

CHAPTER 3

DEFINITION OF CUSTOMER SERVICE

There is no commonly accepted definition for customer service. Furthermore, most authors of customer service books do not offer specific definitions of customer service. Business leaders have long been aware of the business activity called *customer service*; however, as a formal field of study, customer service is young, small, and still developing. Despite the nascent status of the customer service field, one should not be deterred from attempting to define what is being talked about when *customer service* and related terms and phrases are mentioned. It is important to have a working definition of customer service and to understand some of the characteristics of the definition.

Working Definition

Customer Service *is the full range of interactions between a customer and a provider during which time the provider or an environment created by the provider has impact upon the customer and the customer attributes this impact to the provider or to the provider's company.*

This definition is meant to have broad meaning. It is intended to cover the full range of customer service activities all the way from those that are so egregious that they drive new businesses out of business before they have barely gotten started, to those that are so brilliantly outstanding that their providers and their parent companies enjoy widespread fame for their excellence.

When talking about customer service, one does not usually focus upon negative characteristics of providers. The typical focus is upon actions that providers can take that will enhance or improve the delivery of customer service. Providers who are impolite, insensitive, or impatient can greatly damage customer relationships. Long standing business relationships can be totally destroyed by only one or two egregious customer service events.

Sometimes in customer service literature one will see a customer service definition that goes something like this: *Customer service means to do your best to give the customer a delightful experience.* Of course, there is nothing wrong with this statement and it may motivate providers to become better at delivering good customer service; however, neither this statement nor similar statements meet the standard of being good definitions of customer service. The reason they fall short is they tell only half of the story. It is still *customer service* when the provider annoys, irritates, angers, or totally alienates the customer—it's just egregious customer service. When assessing customer service, one needs to see it clearly, whether it's good, or whether it's bad.

Person-to-Person Activity

Customer service is a person-to-person activity. Person-to-person may mean literal *face-to-face* contact, person-to-person on the telephone, or person-to-person in the back and forth of email exchanges. For some companies and some products, the only kind of person-to-person contact that ever occurs is telephone contact or email contact. For example, the person-to-person contact between providers of mail order catalog products and their customers is almost exclusively by telephone or internet.

The essential point is that in most cases of customer service, there must be a personal interaction quality, or an *expectancy of a personal interaction quality* for a customer service event to have occurred. If one writes a letter to a person in a company and gets a letter back in reply to the one that was sent, that is an example of customer service. Also, it should be noted that customer service occurs even when one party of an interactive pair fails to reply. If a customer writes a letter to seek information about a product or to make a complaint and the letter is ignored, one can be assured that an incident of poor customer service will have occurred. The expectancy of *personal interaction quality* is defined by the customer—not the provider.

Distinctions should always be maintained between customer service and the business product that is the very basis for customer service to exist. *The main product of a company is not customer service.* Sometimes a company will describe its main product, or products, using language that makes it sound as though *customer service is the main product.* However, customer service is always directed toward, or attached to, a main product, be it tangible or intangible. Customer service needs a target.

Sometimes important aspects of customer service are delivered so consistently and perfectly that they become absorbed into the definition of the main product. When this happens, everyone takes the main product and its embedded customer-service-like features for granted. They expect that treatments that at a prior time were seen as aspects of *great customer service* are now normal, standard features of the primary product and they may start looking for or demanding something better before being willing to say something represented *Superior Customer Service.* The bar for excellent customer service keeps being lifted higher and higher.

Start of Customer Service

If one has opened a new business, he becomes a customer service provider starting from the very first moment he opens the front door and starts interacting with prospective new customers. One could argue that what the business owner gives at first is only *prospective customer service* and that he cannot give true *customer service* until he has made a sale and created a real customer. Whether or not one insists on being completely technically accurate in his use of the concepts of *customer service*, and *prospective customer service*, it is clear that all customers whether they are *internal, external, primary, secondary, prospective, or potential* should be treated with utmost respect, sensitivity, understanding, and kindness at all times.

Irrespective of how the provider chooses to look at and to use concepts such as *customer service* and *prospective customer service*, he should have full awareness that he does not get to determine whether, when, and where customer service will be offered. If a customer or a prospective customer is around and in the presence of a provider, even the marginal presence, it is the customer or the prospective customer who decides whether a *customer service event* occurred and, if so, whether it was good, bad, inadequate, irrelevant, or commendable.

Customer service occurs potentially every time person-to-person contact occurs between any member of the staff of a provider company and any member of the staff of a customer company. All contacts between staff members of provider companies and customers are opportunities for the provider to create good or poor impressions. And, one should always be aware that customers tend to attribute the tone and the emotion (or the lack of it) of their contacts with any provider to the *entire* provider company. Sometimes customer service activity occurs when the provider is totally unaware that it has occurred. The customer has more to say about whether or not customer service has occurred and whether it was good or bad than does the provider. A personal experience of author Dave Elwood illustrates this point:

> I took my wife to pick up her car from an auto body shop where some dents in a door were fixed and a bumper was replaced. We entered a very small office that included two desks and barely room enough for two folding chairs for guests. The body man who did the work on her car was seated at a desk near to us. As a way of establishing social contact and being politely deferential to him, I said, "*May we sit down?*" I expected he would say something such as "*Certainly,*" or "*Please do.*" However, he said nothing and acknowledged in no way that he had heard me say anything. We sat down anyway. After sitting down, I quickly noticed a sign on the wall of the office touting the highly popular Indianapolis Colts football team. Not to be deterred by the seeming unfriendliness of the body man, I commented, "*Hey, it looks like you have some ball fans around here!*" Again, there was nothing but silence—no reaction, no response, and no acknowledgement that a customer had attempted to interact with a provider.
>
> Since my wife had contacted the provider and made arrangements for the repairs to her car, she and the body man interacted for the next 10-15 minutes working through details of what turned out to be some complicated billing issues. Incidentally, there was no evidence at any time that the body man was hard-of-hearing. During this time, I sat quietly and politely beside her about five feet in front of the body man. At no time did he and I have eye-to-eye contact nor did he speak to me directly or indirectly. After the billing questions were resolved, an invoice was prepared; my wife

wrote a check for the service, we both left the office, and we both drove away in our own separate cars.

To me, this event was a good example of a provider offering egregious customer service (to a *secondary customer* in this case) while, very possibly, being totally unaware that he had alienated a person, a *secondary customer.* I had no reason to think he purposefully directed poor customer service toward me, but, nevertheless, the impact was clearly negative. This gentleman may have been the best auto body repairman for miles around, but in this interaction he diminished chances for his company to receive additional auto body repair business from our family.

Location of Customer Service

Some people think of customer service as an activity that occurs in the front or the back of a store where there is a countertop and an overhead sign that says **Customer Service Department**. It is true that customer service occurs in these settings, but most customer service events occur in other places. Customer service may occur in the parking lot of a department store where a person cleaning the parking lot offers a cheerful greeting to incoming shoppers—many of whom are already customers. Customer service also occurs if the same person is rude to some other visitor.

Customer service may occur in the reception room of an office where a provider such as a salesperson is friendly or clearly unfriendly toward a receptionist. Customer service may occur during a telephone conversation between a customer and a provider. Customer service may occur in the aisle of a department store where a clerk greets a customer with a smile and "*Hello. May I help you?*" Customer service may occur in almost any physical area in a shop, a business, or a factory. Customer service may occur on the premises of the customer or upon the premises of the provider.

At any point, at any place, under any circumstances when a provider comes into contact with a customer for the purpose of dealing with a business issue, customer service occurs. The provider does not say when customer service occurs. It's not something that can be turned on or off very easily. It is mainly the customer who says where customer service occurs. If a customer meets a provider on the street and attempts to address something related to a business transaction, a customer service event will have occurred even if the customer used poor judgment about the venue for the inquiry.

Providers of Customer Service

Each and every member of the staff of a provider company is a potential giver of customer service to external customers and, on a daily basis, gives customer service to internal customer colleagues. *Customer Service* does not need to appear as a box on an organization chart with the implication that it will not happen if someone does not plan for its inclusion. Customer service delivery happens whether one likes it or not and regardless of intentions.

A provider of customer service is any person from the owner of a business down to the newest person hired just yesterday. The reason it is important to say it in these terms is that from the customer's standpoint, anyone connected with the store or a company is a representative or an agent of the owner of a store or an agent of the general management of the company. Therefore, if an attendant in a parking lot is rude to a customer, the customer will likely attribute his negative feelings toward the parking lot attendant all the way up to the owner of the store. The parking lot attendant may protest: "*I didn't mean to do anything that would hurt the ability of the store to do business!*" But the provider, in this case the parking lot attendant, does not get to determine whether or not he renders customer service. Such determinations are solely in the hands of the customer. The customer is in the driver's seat.

Academic Standing of Customer Service

The academic footprint of customer service is small. The smallness of the footprint is dramatically shown by considering two statistics: (a) in 2005-2006, 318,000 students received bachelor's degrees in fields of business (Livingston, 2008), and (b) a Google search performed in 2010 using the phrase "*major in customer service*" found one website (collegetoolkit.washingtonpost.com) that reported only 58 students attending two different colleges (29 per college) had earned bachelor's degrees with majors in *customer service management* in 2007-2008. Another website (collegeboard.com) identified four more bachelor's level colleges that awarded degrees in *customer service management*, but graduation rates for these programs were not shown.

If one were to assume equal graduation rates for the six colleges (6 x 29 = 154), *the total number of customer service management annual graduates would need to* ***more than double to reach just one tenth of one percent*** *(318) of the overall number of business graduates.*

These numbers are no more than approximate estimates of the true number of annual customer service management graduates, but they do make clear that customer service studies constitute an extremely limited slice of today's college curricula. As thinking, writing, theoretical proposals, and empirical research into customer service continue to grow, it is probable that college level courses and majors in customer service will also increase. As businessmen and businesswomen who are in the field and on the firing line everyday become more aware of the importance of customer service issues, such as through reading the *Two Factor Theory of Customer Service*, they will increasingly require that new hires coming from college programs have solid training in how to deliver *Superior Customer Service*.

For those who may lament the neglected state of customer service as a professional discipline worthy of college level study, it may be informative and a source of inspiration to consider the impressive growth that has taken place in the college level study of entrepreneurship. Dr. Donald F. Kuratko, author of *Entrepreneurship: Theory, Process, Practice: Eighth Edition*, the leading college textbook in this area, has noted that 35 years ago college level study of entrepreneurship was virtually non-existent, and that an implicit feeling was that becoming an entrepreneur was for those who could not or did not have a more serious interest in the study of business. Since approximately 1974, there has been a dramatic increase in entrepreneurial studies at the college and university level: now, 600 schools offer majors in entrepreneurial study, there are 300 endowed chairs for entrepreneurial study, 44 professional journals have been launched to disseminate research findings and theory in this area, and 1,600 colleges and universities worldwide offer at least one course in entrepreneurial studies (Kuratko, 2009). What happened in the field of entrepreneurial studies could also happen in the customer service area.

CHAPTER 4

ANALYSIS OF CUSTOMER SERVICE EVENTS

Many discussions of customer service consist of broad generalizations such as *Customer service is good; Customer service is good for business; Everyone should try to give good customer service, etc.* Also, many of these discussions, even discussions among experts in the customer service field, seem not to focus upon questions about the specific nature of *customer service events.* One rarely hears questions such as these: *What are the essential elements or dimensions of customer service events? Do customer service events have a basic shape, structure, or configuration that is mainly true and is applicable from one customer service event to the next customer service event?*

Optimal progress in the customer service field cannot be made without a more detailed inquiry into the nature and structure of *customer service events.* Almost all fields of knowledge that grow and increase in stature represent progressions from broad generalizations, sometimes quite fuzzy and vague, to more specific terms and concepts. There is no reason to expect the customer service field to be different.

Unique Business Behaviors

One way to look at *customer service events* is to see them as parts of an amorphous, loosely knit collection of mainly unique business behaviors that have in common only a few characteristics such as making the customer feel good, solving a problem, or giving the customer a "*wow experience.*" There is nothing wrong with such an understanding of customer service events except that one might wish to ask *Does this approach go far enough? Does it tell us enough about customer service events so as to capture the full range of events or incidents that we may want to place into the customer service category?* The answer is "*No.*" Approaches such as this one do not go far enough. They stop short. When one thinks of the phrase *customer service event*, there should be a deeper more comprehensive understanding of what it means.

Customer Service Events Defined

The phrase *customer service event* is used frequently in the *Two Factor Theory of Customer Service*, but it is not used commonly throughout customer service literature. In the same way that a "working definition" was offered for the broad field of *customer service*, it may be helpful to offer additional explanation and definition for the phrase *customer service event* as it is used within the *Two Factor Theory of Customer Service.*

Customer service events *are perceived as segments of a customer's interactions with a provider, or with environments created by the provider, to which the customer reacts by attributing positive or negative impacts to the provider or to the provider's company. Customer service events may be thought of as the* ***basic building blocks*** *of the broad notion of* ***customer service cultures****. Customer service cultures are populated with infinite numbers of specific* ***customer service events.***

Examples of Customer Service Events

The following three examples help illustrate the meaning of the phrase *customer service event*: ***One***: A customer contacted the "help desk" of a retailer from whom he bought a mobile phone to ask a question about the phone. The person who answered the phone was dismissive toward the caller and advised him to "*read the user's manual*." The entire interaction lasted 20 seconds. The customer expected sympathetic help but was met with rebuff; he was angered. A *customer service event* occurred.

Two: A customer bought a new set of tires for her car. Soon after leaving the tire shop, she discovered one tire had deflated. She called the shop where she bought the tires to report her problem. A service person was dispatched immediately, arrived within five minutes, was apologetic for the problem, was polite to deal with, and replaced the defective tire within 10 minutes. The entire episode from discovery of the deflated tire until the service person drove away was 20 minutes. The customer was pleased with the service. A *customer service event* occurred.

Three: A customer bought a TV set and then discovered on Sunday, one day after the purchase, that the TV had become inoperable. The user's manual for the TV set stated that an 800 number help service was available "*seven days a week*," but the automated voice that answered the customer's call stated that help service was available only "*Monday through Friday*." The customer was annoyed; there was no interaction with another person, but a *customer service event* occurred.

Dimensions of Customer Service Events

To assert that what is called *customer service* is comprised of *customer service events* is a step in the right direction, but the *customer-service-event* concept must be imbued with additional meaning for it to really help advance overall understanding of the *customer service* field.

If a customer service event was good, what made it good? If it was a bad event, what made it bad? If a more complex perception of the nature of customer service events were available, a perception that included different dimensions, one might be able to say "*That particular customer service event was good because of high ratings on dimensions one, two, and three.*" If a customer service event were rated as bad, one might say "*It was bad because of low ratings on dimensions three, five, and six.*" In the current state of affairs in the field of customer service, it is not possible to make such statements because there are no commonly accepted dimensions that could help provider's to know the *composition, structure,* or *shape* of *customer service events.*

Few or Many Dimensions

It is worthy to strive for a deeper understanding of *customer service events,* but could one try so hard to catalog everything and to explain everything that he would end up with so many concepts, characteristics, and dimensions that things would be made more complicated and confusing rather than to be made more simple and clear? Author Dave Elwood believes the answer is "*Yes.*" One should go beyond the two or three characteristics that would qualify a business event to fit into the *customer service event* category, but should stop short of a burdensome, complicated system that would attempt to answer too many questions.

The Seven Dimension Structure

Within the *Two Factor Theory of Customer Service,* ***customer service events*** were assumed to be measurable, or ratable, along seven different dimensions. These seven dimensions comprised the structure of customer service events. The dimensions were chosen based on the judgment of *Two Factor Theory of Customer Service* author Dave Elwood, not upon mathematical or scientific analyses that would give them status as independent factors or dimensions of customer service events. Nevertheless, they are a start; they are a beginning.

The selected dimensions were felt to be both sufficiently broad to capture the majority of things that one would say are *customer service events* while, at the same time, being sufficiently narrow and specific to avoid excessively overlapping meanings. The dimensions refer to aspects of *customer service events* that make customers want to say a service event was good, or was bad.

The dimensions are: *Accessible, Temporal, Emotional, Informational, Aptitudinal, Solutional,* and *Relational.* The meanings of these seven dimensions are explored in detail in the following seven chapters.

Use of the word "*structure*" could imply that something of a physical, tangible nature was being attributed to customer service events: such implication is not intended. The word "*structure*" is used only as a literary device to convey that dimensions of *customer service events* are perceived as hanging together, clustering together, or as having a common focus within the framework of the *Two Factor Theory of Customer Service.*

When customer service is good, it's good for specific reasons, and when it's bad, it's bad for specific reasons. What the seven dimension structure offers is a concept, or a methodology, that enables providers to have a richer, more comprehensive understanding of just what it is that happens when a customer service event is good, and what happens when it is not so good, or is very poor. Having such knowledge can help providers see steps to take to make things better—to work toward the high standard of routinely providing *Superior Customer Service,* and routinely finding higher profits.

Residence of Dimensions

Do the dimensions attributed to customer service events reside in a particular location? Are they in the customer, in the provider, in the interactions between customers and providers, in some other psychological or physical space, or in no space at all? Persuasive arguments could be put forth supporting each possibility. It is assumed within the *Two Factor Theory of Customer Service* that dimensions of customer service events abide within the provider, or, perhaps more appropriately worded, are *associated with the provider.* A potential advantage of seeing the dimensions from this perspective is that such a view may make it easier for providers to make changes, in their own behavior or in the environment, which could improve customer service.

Ratable Provider-Customer Interactions

A given *customer service event* could be important on only one or two dimensions, but could be important on three or four dimensions, or more. It is the position of the *Two Factor Theory of Customer Service* that for a customer to see an interaction with a provider as a *customer service event*, the event must be ratable on at least one of the seven dimensions of customer service. Ratings, of course, would be ratings made by the customer.

As examples of ratable customer service events, the main perceptions of a customer may have been that the provider was *very easy to get hold of*—**high** on the *accessibility dimension*; to another customer, it was the provider's *in depth product knowledge* that caught his attention—**high** on the *informational dimension*; still another customer noticed and was uplifted by the *positive emotion* exuded by the provider and the seeming ease with which he *resolved an intractable problem*—**high** on the *emotional dimension* and **high** on *solutional dimension*; and, finally, a customer may have noticed the *fundamental likability* of the provider ("*I could be friends with this person!*"), the provider's ability to express *in depth understanding of the customer's main concerns*, and, in contrast to two positives, a negative—frustration that a *service expected to take 10 minutes took one full hour*—**high** on the *relational dimension*, **high** on the *informational dimension*, and **low** on the *temporal dimension*.

Other Systematic Frameworks

Ron Kaufman (2012), in his book titled *Uplifting Service*, approached customer service in a way similar to the approach used by *Two Factor Theory of Customer Service* author Dave Elwood. Kaufman described natural sequences of interactions having a beginning, middle, and end as "*Service Transactions.*" For example, buying a piece of office equipment, having it delivered, having it installed, and later calling a repairman for service would all be separate "*Service Transactions.*" He described "*Perception Points*" as the "*moments when people* (customers) *experience your service and form their opinions*" about it. "*Perception Points*" may be "*mapped*" along "*sensory processes*" (seeing, hearing, etc.) and along "*themes:*" people, products, packaging, locations, promotions, policies, and processes.

Elwood's "*customer service events*" may be assessed along seven different "*dimensions.*" "*Customer service events*" occur when a customer reacts to some aspect of a provider's behavior, or an environment created by the provider, and attributes positive or negative impacts to it. Kaufman's "*Perception Points*" and author Elwood's "*customer service events*" appear to share some common functions. Kaufman and Elwood have presented disciplined, systematic approaches to understanding specific acts of customer service. While there is similarity, Kaufman's approach to understanding customer service and the *Two Factor Theory of Customer Service* are separate, independent systems.

Other authors have also offered systematic frameworks for understanding and advancing customer service practices. For example, Berry (1995) outlined five broad "*dimensions*" based on "*qualitative and empirical research*" performed by him and colleagues that customers used to "*judge service quality*." The dimensions were "*Reliability, Tangibles, Responsiveness, Assurance, and Empathy*." And, Whiteley & Hessan (1996) described "*five proven strategies*" for becoming a truly "*customer centered* " company: 1) develop a laser-beam focus upon targeted customers, 2) "*hardwire*" what customers say they want to what is delivered to customers, 3) stress "*universal collaboration*" where everyone at every level helps connect to customers, 4) strive to move from "*mere customer satisfaction to outright customer enthusiasm*," and 5) move from "*facilitative leadership*" where one empowers others to do the work and then watches to "*contact leadership*" where leaders "*work every day out in the trenches*" so that fellow employees may have clear pictures of their roles and be excited about what is possible in the future.

Also, many authors have focused upon *company cultures* as a way to understand customer service (e.g., Basch, 2002). All approaches are legitimate and productive, depending upon the needs of a particular provider or a particular company, and wisdom may be adopted from one approach or from several approaches.

CHAPTER 5

CUSTOMER SERVICE DIMENSION: ACCESSIBLE

The accessible dimension, checked in Text Box 5-1, concerns the entire array of situations, circumstances, and conditions that may enhance or limit *customer initiated contacts* with providers. Accessibility is about the customer getting into contact with the provider in person, via phone, email, the U.S. postal service, or electronic social media. Accessibility may concern the location, layout, or size of an office, or the days, hours, and starting-stopping times of operation. Accessibility may concern anything that enhances, eases, or helps, or frustrates, blocks, or deters a customer from getting into touch with a provider.

Dimensions of Customer Service Events
▶ Accessible
Temporal
Emotional
Informational
Aptitudinal
Solutional
Relational

Text Box 5-1

High accessibility means that the provider has done everything that is practically possible to make it simple, convenient, handy, clear, and hassle free for the customer to make contact with the provider. The customer is made to feel wanted and accepted.

Low accessibility means the opposite. Customers are made to feel that providers, through intention, indifference, incompetence, or preservation of convenience for themselves, do things that leave customers feeling frustrated, blocked, thwarted, or impeded in their efforts to get into touch with providers. Accessibility has to do with it being easy for customers to contact providers—it has little or nothing to do with how easy it is for providers to get into touch with customers. The accessibility dimension of customer service is complex. Each business has a different set of accessibility needs.

Physical Accessibility

Physical accessibility is easy to understand. An office or business located on street level with an entry door near a sidewalk is more accessible than a third floor office in a building with no elevator. A determined customer will find his way to the third floor office, but all other things being equal, many customers and potential customers will opt for the first floor office, the one that is most accessible.

Elwood Staffing considered potential office space in the downtown of a city of about 10,000 people. The space was not ideal, but it could have worked. However, a decision was made against the space because it did not include dedicated parking spaces for staff, visitors, and job applicants. Lack of parking would have impeded accessibility. Finding parking space near the office, come rain or shine, would be a hit or miss experience. The office space finally chosen included a fully adequate parking lot.

Other external considerations such as street location, visibility from the street, traffic islands that prevent turns, and signage restrictions can all affect accessibility. In its early years, Elwood Staffing was located in a medical complex on a busy state highway. There was no signage that could be seen from the highway. Highway lanes were separated by a concrete divider strip that made it impossible for one lane of traffic to turn directly into the parking lot. Not surprisingly, complaints were made by job applicants, *secondary customers*, who "*drove around*" trying to find the Elwood Staffing office.

The importance of physical accessibility for an office or business can vary dramatically with the type of business. A fast food restaurant needs high visibility and good parking. Decisions to eat in particular fast food restaurants are often made on impulse. If it's not easy to get into the parking lot of one restaurant, another restaurant a halfblock down the street will serve just as well. Without easy accessibility, competitive advantages will be lost. The accessibility needs for a drive-through-drop-off dry cleaning company would be quite different: a small to medium sized parking lot, modest signage, an easy to reach drive-through-drop-off window, and convenient hours of operation so that one could drop things off early in the morning on the way to work and pick them up after hours on the way back home.

In marked contrast to restaurants and dry cleaners, the office location of a medical specialist (a provider) seeing patients (customers) only by appointment, may not be as important. Patients (customers) are highly motivated to see their providers—they will not be deterred from finding the right office.

Hours and Days of Operation

When one thinks of *Superior Customer Service*, hours and days of operation are not usually the first things that pop into a person's mind. For many businesses, hours and days of operation are standardized as 8:00 am to 5:00 pm, or 9:00 am to 5:00 pm, Monday through Friday. Typically, neither hours nor days when a business is open are seen as aspects of business operation that could be adjusted to gain competitive advantages or to create opportunities for giving better customer service. Nevertheless, one should keep an open mind regarding the possibility of changing things as fundamental as schedules for opening and closing.

Depending upon the nature of one's business, the more days per week it is open the more convenient and friendly it may seem to the customer. The same is true for hours of operation. For some types of businesses, it is friendlier to the customer if a store opens a little earlier and stays open a little later than what might be normally expected.

Practical considerations play a big role in determining the days and hours of operation of a business. In some types of businesses, trying to stay open more than five days per week or trying to keep expanded hours of operation would make absolutely no business sense. The main thing for a provider to keep in mind is the question: *What would make good sense for my customers and what steps can I take that would be practical and would help me accommodate my customers?* For example, if there would be subtle push from customers for added hours of operation, or if the provider would notice an overlooked advantage that could be won by different hours of operation, he should consider changing his hours of operation. At the end of the day, whatever is done must make practical sense and must be profitable.

As banking industry regulations have loosened over the years and as competition has increased, the hours when banks are open have become more accommodating to ordinary customers. It used to be quite common to hear people refer to *"banker's hours"* when they wished to make the point that another person wanted to work only at times that were fully convenient to him or her. Now, one seldom hears that expression because banks try very hard to accommodate their customers—no more Wednesday afternoon closures, more flexible weekday hours, and Saturday morning hours.

Similar changes have come about in the health care industry. As competition has increased in some sectors of medical practice, it has become more common to see expanded hours of operation such as early morning walk-in hours, some evening hours, and Saturday morning hours. What these changes mean is that health care providers have been attempting to adjust to the challenges of greater competition by being more sensitive to and more accessible to the needs of their patient-customers. Another aspect of this increased accessibility is that physicians are now more willing to make their home phone numbers available to patients than was true in the 1960's and earlier. The lesson for customer service providers is to be highly sensitive to the needs and desires of customers for more convenient and accessible terms of contact.

Telephone Accessibility

Telephones are woven into the fabric of all commerce and human interaction. They are an essential part of business. Given the ubiquity of telephones, here are four suggestions to improve telephone accessibility.

First, make sure that enough incoming lines are available to handle the anticipated volume of calls coming into an office. Also, make sure that adequate personnel are available to answer the phones. No customer likes to receive repeated busy signals. Telephones should be answered promptly, and, as much as possible, a live person should answer.

Second, providers need to publish, quite openly and widely, the numbers that customers may use to reach them. Catalog sales companies have learned this lesson well. Some catalogs include the company's toll free number, in large bold print, at the bottom of each page of the catalog. These providers are trying to make themselves fully accessible to the customer. They don't want to take the chance that anything could interfere with the customer's impulse to buy. If the customer has to spend time searching through a catalog to find the provider's telephone number, something could happen: someone could knock on the door, the phone could ring, the customer could recall an errand he needed to run, or something else could distract the customer from dialing the number and completing the order.

Third, Internet Protocol (IP) based telephone systems are growing rapidly and must be seen as avenues of accessibility that have something to offer that goes beyond what is offered by regular landline systems. Here are two potential advantages having customer service implications. First, for companies with offices in different cities and states, IP phone systems make contacting a colleague in another state as easy as contacting a colleague just a few doors down the hallway. *Internal* to *internal customer service* may be facilitated. Second, IP phone systems create the possibility of integrating landline phone systems, mobile phones, appointment-meeting calendars, telephone usage records, and message-greeting options for enhanced flexibility and immediacy of helpfulness when calls are received from *external customers*. The fewer the hassles that a customer must deal with when he tries to contact a provider, the happier he is likely to be.

Fourth, Sophisticated, automated telephone answering systems that are found in almost all businesses have made it easy for customers to leave "voice mail" messages for providers. Sometimes, voice mail messages are answered within minutes after a customer has left the message. That is good customer service. Voice mail boxes should be monitored frequently. Unfortunately, some providers are not conscientious about monitoring their voice mail boxes. In their minds, they are too busy performing other *highly important tasks* to check voice mail boxes and to return calls—the customer can wait until it's convenient for the provider to return the call. To the degree that happens, a provider has been inaccessible; he has provided poor customer service.

While there are clear advantages to modern telephone technology, the downsides cannot be overlooked. *Who has not called an office or a company with a simple question to ask and been forced to listen to several layers of recorded messages that were irrelevant, time consuming, and that created so much frustration that hanging up and starting over seemed like the only sensible thing to do?* Telephone answering systems are indeed appropriate in many situations and they may save a provider some money by sparing the cost of live people to answer the telephone, but there is a price to pay. The price, of course, is diminished customer service.

Albrecht & Zemke (2003) clearly recognized the detrimental impact that automated telephone technology could have on customer service. They noted: "*It's impossible to call a big company and talk to a human being. You get a telephone menu … The mindless use of digital technology to depopulate the customer interface will turn out to be one of the biggest mistakes many companies will ever make.*" Excessive reliance upon automated telephone technology is present in small companies as well as big companies. One wonders if reliance on automated telephone technology by small companies is sometimes motivated by the belief that it will make them appear to be big companies, so big and successful that sophisticated answering systems are needed to handle the large volume of calls they receive! Unless the cost cannot be justified, live people should always answer the telephone.

Beemer (Beemer & Shook, 2009; p. 29), founder and CEO of America's Research Group, a consumer research firm, reported that 97.6% of people calling for information or service "*prefer speaking to a live person*" rather than interacting with an automated telephone system. Timm (2001) made this comment about automated telephone systems: "*Of the many credit cards I carry, my favorites are the American Express Card and Discover Private Issue. I perceive higher intrinsic value in these two products for two reasons: They give me airline miles or cash back, and when I need to call either of these providers I can speak to a live person almost immediately. Other cards linger in my wallet because, when I have a problem, they force me through a maze of telephone switching that is annoying and time-consuming. This live person contact enhances my perception of intrinsic value.*"

Internet Accessibility

In the last twenty years, the internet has become almost as thoroughly integrated into business operations as has the telephone. Virtually all large businesses, those with annual revenue over $500 million, have extensive internet presences. A September 2008 report showed that 84 percent of companies with revenue from $10 million to $500 million had websites, and that 69 percent of companies with annual revenue from $1.0 million to $2.49 million had websites. Seventy-nine percent of small businesses shop "online" on a regular basis. A July 2006 report from *shop.org* stated that online sales were growing from 20 to 25 percent annually. Given the rapid growth of the internet, the true numbers for 2013 are probably much greater.

How does this explosive increase in internet usage impact customer service issues?

First, websites have become so commonplace that many potential customers now search the internet when they want to find a place of business, or wish to make product comparisons, rather than to search first in a telephone book, or drive a car from store to store. For some customers and potential customers, failure of a company to maintain an internet website is equal to that company saying: *For those of you who have some technological sophistication and* *choose to use the internet, I'm not interested in your business. I choose to be inaccessible to you.*

Second, the ease with which visitors can navigate a website and the information they find on the website can encourage them to return to the website, or make them resolute against ever again returning to the website. Some website visitors hope to gain nothing more than basic information about a company such as physical location and telephone number, yet they wind up totally frustrated. The information was present on the website, but was so difficult to find that the *potential customer* wasted valuable time exploring dead ends. In other cases, the information was missing altogether. For *Two Factor Theory of Customer Service* author Dave Elwood, a rule of thumb is to only do business with companies that are willing to reveal their physical addresses and telephone numbers on their websites. For those companies unwilling to publicize this information, it is as though they are saying: "*I don't want you to know my physical location and I don't want you to bother me with phone calls in case you have questions or problems with my goods or services. I am quite willing to limit my accessibility to you.*"

Third, selling goods and services over the internet dramatically highlights the need for clearly defined and easy to use procedures. The easier it is for a user to interact with a website, the more accessible the website. Customers do not like to make repeated entries before they *finally get it right*. Customers who frequently order on the internet have few problems. But, the problem is that many customers are "*first time*" buyers and may be just "*one time*" buyers. For these types of buyers, the online buying process needs to be *abundantly clear and easy to use from the very start*. The easier it is to order online, the more *accessible* the provider; the more accessible the provider, the more likely a one time buyer will become a frequent buyer.

Procedural Barriers

Some internet based businesses, in the spirit of attempting to collect helpful marketing information, ask potential customers to fill in forms and provide personal data—sometimes before allowing them to browse their websites. Both potential customers and real customers see such data collection efforts as annoying and intrusive. Such practices amount to procedural barriers. The provider holds the *customer* or *potential customer* "at arm's length."

Customers want to skip all forms and procedures that they can legitimately avoid. Data collection efforts should be limited to clearly necessary information. Providers have great control over their accessibility to customers. Providers should do all within their power that is reasonable and practical to convey to *customers* and *potential customers* that contacting them is easy, quick, simple, and convenient.

CHAPTER 6

CUSTOMER SERVICE DIMENSION: TEMPORAL

The *temporal* dimension, checked in Text Box 6-1, concerns the time frame within which customer service is provided. In general, good time frames imply prompt responses, or, at worst, only short delays. Customer service provided quickly is usually seen as good customer service.

How soon one looks at a customer, smiles, shows a pleasant expression, speaks to the customer, or starts providing some kind of service is usually a sign of good customer service. In marked contrast to prompt service, customer service that is slow, late, delayed, tardy, delinquent, lagging, or sluggish is often seen as poor or bad customer service.

Dimensions of Customer Service Events
Accessible
▶ Temporal
Emotional
Informational
Aptitudinal
Solutional
Relational

Text Box 6-1

The very general concept *temporal* was chosen (rather than *quick, prompt,* or *fast*) to describe the time dimension for customer service because the impact of both short and long time frames needs to be understood. The *temporal dimension* applies just as much to *atrociously bad customer service*—service delivered extremely delinquently—as it does to *superbly outstanding customer service*—service given so swiftly as to surprise and deeply please the customer. Slow or fast, it is still customer service. All customer service delivery fits into time frames. Customer service that is slow, late, and never on time is still customer service—it is *poor customer service.* Swift, prompt, responsive customer service is the kind of customer service that is usually the best and the kind that a provider likes to think about, talk about, and strive to deliver.

Acknowledging

When a customer enters an office, one of the most effective things one can do to setup positive expectancies is to quickly acknowledge the customer's presence. Some customers are quite tolerant when they are not immediately attended to, but other customers are clearly annoyed when it seems they are being ignored. A person who is greeting visitors does not always need to suspend all other activity, regardless of its importance, to greet visitors, but making eye contact with a visitor and signaling that one will get to the person momentarily is always well received.

Sensing Customer Expectancies

There are few things a provider can do that make a better impression on a customer than to attend to him or her promptly and to meet his or her requests quickly. But, it needs to be acknowledged that some customers are quite relaxed and leisurely in their approach to shopping and buying. To some customers, the idea of going out to buy something is more of a social, relational experience than it is an errand to quickly acquire a highly needed product or service. Providers need to be wise enough to know when customers are interested in *quick service* versus more relaxed, *unhurried service.*

For example, a woman customer in a dress shop could be annoyed if she felt that a salesperson (a provider) were too focused upon helping her reach a decision on what to buy, ringing up the sale, wrapping up the purchase, and getting the customer out the door rather to be patient while the customer decides just which dress it is that best meets her tastes and needs. In sharp contrast, a man who has gone to a hardware store to pick up plumbing supplies to fix a water leakage problem at his home may be laser focused upon finding the right parts, paying for them, and getting out of the store quickly. For him, going to the hardware store is an errand to be run, not a social experience. No matter how well a provider understands the general principles of good customer service, few things are more important than to know the interests and motives of the customer.

Orienting

Some aspects of how one interacts with customers are quite subtle but also quite important. If one has the significant responsibility of being the first person to greet a visitor in an office, he or she needs to be keenly aware of how visitors will react and what they will notice about how they are received. If one is sitting at a desk working on a computer when a visitor first appears, different reactions are possible. If one remains oriented toward the computer, turns the torso slightly, tilts the head up slightly, and rolls his or her eyes up just enough to see the visitor's face, then a poor job will have been done of welcoming the visitor. Performance such as this would convey to a visitor that neither the provider nor the company was glad to see the visitor. What one would be saying would be: *I am doing some work on the computer that is really important to me; your presence is intrusive, and the quicker I can get rid of you the happier I'll be.*

For those responsible for receiving visitors, what should be done when a visitor appears? One should promptly turn toward the visitor, raise head and torso, look the visitor straight in the face, and greet the person warmly. The whole process should occur reasonably quickly. Such behavior would convey to the visitor that both the provider and the company were happy that this person has come to their office. For the most part, such behavior is appropriate even when there is high likelihood that the visitor is not a *customer,* perhaps just a salesperson.

Answering the Telephone Promptly

In general, the more quickly a telephone is answered the better. When telephones are answered slowly, only after four, five, or more rings, what it often means is that the person receiving calls is so busy with other callers and other tasks that new calls cannot be answered in a timely manner. However, that is not always the case. There are people serving in *first-contact* customer service roles that are responsible for answering all incoming phone calls, but who seem totally oblivious to the need to answer the telephone promptly. There is only one way to look at such behavior: it is *poor customer service.*

Customers feel their time is valuable. They have other things to do. They may become frustrated if the telephone *wait-time* is too long. Furthermore, when *customers* leave voice mail messages, they want them answered quickly. The same is true for many email messages. Important business decisions and information are delivered multiple times daily, even in small businesses. Responding promptly and following rules of etiquette should apply here as well. It is one thing to try to keep one's email box cleared of *"spam,"* and it is an entirely different matter to be careless about how one handles legitimate email-based business correspondence. Strive to be courteous, prompt, and positive with both *external* and *internal customers.*

Filling Staffing Orders

People who work in the staffing industry understand that one of the most important requirements in this field is to *fill orders promptly.* When an order comes to an Elwood Staffing office, each person in the office does everything possible to see that the order is filled quickly. It is often true that customers may have no more than three or four days of lead time before needing to contact a staffing company to order 20, 30, or 40 new workers to arrive at their companies within a few days. When orders such as these come through, the customer does not want to hear: "*It will take us three weeks to find this many qualified workers.*" The customer wants action now and if the numbers of workers needed within the time frames specified cannot be provided, the customer may look to another staffing company to fill the need. And, usually, the other company is more than happy to try to meet the customer's need. Rush orders have never caused Elwood Staffing to demur.

In addition to wanting workers on short notices, most customers that use staffing services want workers to be free of illegal drugs, free of felony convictions, experienced, reliable, and well-adjusted. The customer wants all of these things and Elwood Staffing does its best to meet the requests of the customer within agreed time frames.

Meeting Customer Timing Demands

It is important to understand that in the staffing industry (and probably most other industries) it is the customer who sets the timing expectancies for when a job needs to be done. Most customers are reasonable concerning their requests and they recognize that practical realities must be taken into account when estimating how quickly a job can be done. But, one cannot be too tightly bound by practical realities. Sometimes, extraordinary steps are required to meet the needs of the customer.

Some customers make demands that are impossible to meet. If this happens, it is better to acknowledge that an order cannot be filled on time than to promise the work will be done and then fail to perform. When work can be done quickly, whether or not quick turnaround was requested by the customer, it is best to go ahead and do it rather than to "*take one's sweet time*" to get the job done. The word *promptitude* is appropriate in this context. It is not found in some dictionaries, but it is a word having laser sharp meaning: *the characteristic of doing things without delay*. Everyone who is truly customer-oriented should appreciate the word *promptitude*.

Flexibility in Applying the Temporal Dimension

Probably everyone has heard complaints against medical doctors for working too hard to wrap things up and get the patient our of the door as opposed to more fully accepting the patient, hearing what is on his or her mind, and allowing the patient to feel some sense of closure before the appointment comes to an end. To patients, the *temporal dimension* of good customer service applies to the appointment *starting on time*, not *ending quickly*.

Cultural expectancies and standards may play a big role in how one thinks about and tries to apply the temporal dimension to customer service questions. The first time author Dave Elwood traveled abroad, he made a telephone call back to the U.S.A. After some effort, he got into touch with a long distance operator, but was then "*put on hold*." Being put on hold was acceptable, except the "*hold*" lasted 10 to 20 minutes. It was not clear if the line were dead, if the call had been forgotten, or if the delay were "perfectly normal." The call was finally completed, but there was a strong feeling of being frustrated and thinking: *being on hold for 10 to 20 minutes and not knowing if the line is* ***dead*** *or* ***alive*** *is not good customer service*. Part of the problem was that Elwood did not know what was normal in the country he was visiting. With a bias toward doing things promptly, wise providers strive to become aware of the various considerations that could modify how the temporal dimension affects delivery of *Superior Customer Service.*

CHAPTER 7

CUSTOMER SERVICE DIMENSION: EMOTIONAL

The emotional dimension, checked in Text Box 7-1, is meant to cover nearly the entire range of human emotions. Customer-provider interactions may range all the way from the customer feeling hurt or humiliated and vowing never to do business with that provider again to the customer being absolutely delighted because he or she has just been *"wowed"* by a customer- service-provider *superstar* (see Peters, 1994). The range of situations evoking emotional reactions that either draw customers to providers or repulse them is infinite. Service providers and salespeople have emotions, but emotional reactions within the customer are the most important emotions. The goal, as much as possible, is for customers to feel good about their contacts with providers.

> **Dimensions of Customer Service Events**
>
> Accessible
> Temporal
> ▶ Emotional
> Informational
> Aptitudinal
> Solutional
> Relational

Text Box 7-1

The emotional dimension concerns putting the customer at ease, pleasing the customer, and creating feelings of delight. It is usually a positive sign when a customer feels relaxed, comfortable, and confident following a meeting with a provider. Providers vary greatly in their effectiveness at making customers feel good. Some providers are uncanny in their ability to come up with precisely correct, fitting, and sensitive remarks that make other people feel uplifted, accepted, and happy to be in the presence of the provider. Other providers seem, without even trying, to rub people the wrong way, to create awkward situations, or to create unpleasant emotions in those with whom they interact. A provider can be trained to become more sensitive to nuances of behavior that affect customers and all other people as well.

Significance of Emotional Dimension

How important is the emotional dimension of customer service? One way to approach this question is to compare the emotional dimension with other dimensions of customer service. The *accessibility* dimension of customer service may be handled so poorly (he is never around and won't return calls) that one's business may fail, but customers would not necessarily have strong negative feelings against the provider. Customers may attribute inaccessibility to poor planning, lack of funds, or lack of experience in business.

A customer may have similar reactions to *temporal* dimension failures. When things are not done in a timely manner, customers may be frustrated and annoyed; they may even take their business to another provider, but they do not necessarily have strong, negative feelings against the provider who failed to give timely service. Rather than to have strong feelings against providers who give slow, tardy service, customers are likely to dismiss them as simply incompetent. Then, they take their business to other providers.

The scenario is quite different when it comes to the *emotional* dimension of customer service. If a service provider has acted in a dismissive, rude, or insulting manner toward a customer, has upset the customer on the *emotional dimension*, one can be certain the customer will react strongly and will remember the incident. The customer may affirm never again to enter that store, or never again to deal with that provider. And, deeply offended customers usually make sure all of their friends hear about their bad experiences. Blackshaw (2008) made the point dramatically in the title of his book: *Satisfied Customers Tell Three Friends, Angry Customers Tell 3,000.* "Angry" internet messages posted in strategic locations may be viewed by hundreds or thousands of people within minutes or hours after their postings.

While on the staff of a community mental health center, author Dave Elwood performed *National Institute of Mental Health* sponsored research. One time, a special piece of air conditioning equipment was needed for a psychological testing room. It was unclear how best to describe the needed equipment or who a likely supplier could be. It was decided to start by visiting a local appliance store that sold window air conditioners and whose owner had an industrial background. As it happened, the owner of the store was present and offered to help. After an attempt was made to describe the needed equipment to the store owner, he advised he could not help and that the approach being made to the problem was "*asinine*." He was thanked for his opinion and never contacted again. No attempt was made to *spread the word* about the *poor customer service* received, but the store owner successfully *slammed the door* on any future business from the mental health center.

A provider need not go so far as to insult a customer or potential customer for the person to become miffed. Some customers are willing to turn their attention elsewhere if a provider is only mildly dismissive of their inquiry, or is only slightly insensitive to their feelings. Wise providers are always on the lookout for ways to create positive emotions in customers.

Ideal Standard for Emotional Dimension

What standard should be expected for the emotional dimension of customer service? If each customer who comes into contact with a provider could go away feeling *wonderful*, that would be good, but it would not be realistic to expect such an outcome for each provider-customer contact. If each customer who comes into contact with a provider could go away with a *conscious awareness of feeling just a little good*, that would be desirable, but even that level of emotion may be too much to expect.

An ideal standard for the *emotional dimension* would be for each provider to make each customer happy, and to delight customers as often as possible. *But, an* ***attainable and reasonable standard*** *would be for each provider to strive to create in each customer feelings that are at least neutral and, hopefully, tilt toward the positive end of the emotional continuum.* Amaze and delight as often as possible, but make sure each customer goes away with a leaning or a bias toward positive feelings and opinions no matter how mild, subtle, or subliminal those feelings and opinions may be. Customers tend to be accepting and forgiving when they feel providers exude positive feelings toward them, try to understand their problems, enjoy their presences, and are willing to accommodate their particular issues.

Creating Positive Emotions

Providers can do many things to help customers feel good. These actions are easy to understand, require minimal training, and they are not large budget items. When a *customer* or a *prospective customer* and a provider first meet, the provider can look directly at the person and smile. That simple gesture conveys to customers that their mere presence has created positive emotions in the provider and that they are welcome. To look and to smile is a good way to react if the customer initiated the contact or if the provider initiated contact. It does not matter who initially made the contact happen.

Once a person has smiled at the customer, he or she can say something such as *Thank you for coming to our company. How may I help you?* Or, if the provider requested the meeting, he or she might say "*Thank you for agreeing to meet me. The main reason I want to meet . . .*"

Depending on the circumstance, one could invite the person to be seated and ask if anything could be done to make him or her feel comfortable. Sometimes, the simple act of offering a glass of water, cup of coffee, or soft drink is greatly appreciated. Of course, there can be no general prescription for things to say and to do that will fit all situations. Good judgment and common sense must be used so that what is said and done is fitting, appropriate, and likely to be accepted by the person to whom one is speaking.

While specific words and actions cannot be prescribed that will fit all situations, there are certain ways of responding that are almost always appropriate regardless of the time, the setting, the people, the purpose, the circumstances, or anything else (Willingham, 1992). *What are these ways of responding?* When meeting a customer, it is almost always appropriate to do any of the following:

- smile or show a pleasant expression
- look directly at the customer when addressing her
- say "Thank you" and "Please"
- show respect
- be polite and courteous
- appreciate the customer's willingness to meet with you
- show appropriate deference to the customer (he or she is your boss!)
- accommodate the customer's wants and needs

- be understanding toward the customer
- be helpful and try to solve the customer's problems
- attempt to see things from the customer's point of view

Doing such things is usually helpful, but these actions alone are not guarantees that positive emotions will be created. If a customer has angrily approached a provider to complain about a failure in the provider's product, a substantial part of restoring good feelings in the customer will be to fix the problem. Being polite and respectful toward the customer is probably a good way to start a meeting, but these actions need to be supplemented by other actions that demonstrate to the customer that the provider understands the problem and is an effective problem solver, or knows the steps to take assuring that another person will solve the problem.

Erasing Negative Emotions

Negative emotions in a customer are not just undesirable and unfortunate. Significant negative emotions ("significant" can be very small) can destroy the customer-provider relationship. Given the importance of the emotional dimension of customer service, providers should do all they can to create positive emotions and to correct or erase negative emotions.

Sometimes negative emotions can be observed to be developing in the customer right on the spot in real time. When this happens, the provider should act quickly to correct things. If the customer has failed to understand something, the provider should apologize promptly and should patiently allow the customer to share his "misunderstood perception." Then, the provider should offer additional explanation that can clarify things. If a provider has said something while trying to handle the customer's problem that has confused, annoyed, or angered the customer, the provider should try to assure the customer that understanding his or her issues and retaining his or her good will are of utmost importance to the provider. In circumstances such as these, providers should not move forward until everything reasonable has been done to restore positive feelings in the customer.

One of the most challenging problems in trying to deal with negative emotions or negative mind sets in customers is that often times they will not say how they feel or think. At least they will not tell how they feel with their lips. What they do is to say how they feel with their feet. They walk away from one business and walk into the front door of another business. Frequently, the other business is the provider's competition. Many customers don't want to be bothered with explaining that they are unhappy and why they are unhappy. How customers behave when they are dissatisfied varies dramatically from retail settings to business-to-business settings. In business-to-business settings, customers are much more willing to say when they are dissatisfied with something. However, even business customers don't always say how they feel and what they are thinking until it's too late for the provider to react.

Rosenbluth & Peters (2002) told about losing an $80 million account. The loss came as a complete surprise and was "*devastating*." Furthermore, even the customer agreed that Rosenbluth's firm had provided outstanding customer service. When the facts became known, it was clear that what happened was the customer went with another provider that gave lower pricing. One lesson to learn from the Rosenbluth experience is that one should stay close to the customer. Make few assumptions about how the customer feels about the business relationship between you and him. Regularly probe all aspects of one's relationships with customers. If a sensitive, problematic area is found, make a sincere attempt to alleviate the stress and check back soon to see how well the action was received by the customer.

When a customer does share unhappiness or anger, or even a simple lack of enthusiasm for some aspect of service, that customer presents a *golden* opportunity to the provider to salvage a business relationship. In such cases, the provider needs *to go all out* to try to solve the problem, to absolve the customer of blame, and to restore a positive feeling and mind set in the customer. *Why is the opportunity golden?* Goodman (2009) reported research showing that "*In almost all business sectors, a customer who complains and is satisfied by the resolution of his complaint is actually 30 percent more loyal than a non-complainer* ..." Furthermore, Goodman reported that "*Getting three non-complaining customers* ***to complain*** *(i.e., to openly and sincerely share any frustrations they may have) and satisfying them produces the same revenue as winning one new customer.*"

Unfortunately, some providers see complaints by customers as *battles that the provider must win*, as *opportunities for the provider to straighten out the customer's wrongheaded thinking*, or as *contests to see if the provider can out smart or out maneuver the customer.* Of course, none of these attitudes are productive. What they do is destroy provider-customer relationships and drive customers away for good.

Subtlety of Emotional Dimension

One cannot fully appreciate the significance of the emotional dimension of customer service until understanding that most of the differences between providers giving great customer service versus providers giving poor customer service are, in reality, very small. One way to grasp this important fact is to look at sports analogies. In championship golf, after spending four days playing eighteen holes per day, the tournament winner may not be decided until the very last hole, the 18th hole, that the champion wins with a birdie while all of his or her opponents had to settle for pars. In track meets, the person who wins no medal may be less than one tenth of a second slower than the person who wins the gold medal. The famous *Indianapolis 500* auto race has been won, after 500 miles of driving, by less than one car length. The analogies could go on and on.

The same thing that is true in the world of sports is true in the world of customer service. The winners and the losers are often separated by the smallest of margins. Those who become legendary leaders in providing great customer service keep on and keep on doing very small things better and better. Their competitors fail to see the importance of what is happening. By keeping on doing small things better and better, the leaders out distance their competitors and when the chips are down, they win by a nose.

Companies that provide poor customer service do not have policies that their providers must annoy, offend, anger, or insult at least one customer per day! Far from it, companies whose providers give poor customer service may have *Standard Operating Procedure Manuals* that extol the value of good customer service and may even outline how to go about delivering such service. Typically, those companies and their providers do not do outlandish things to drive customers away—although outlandish things do happen. What happens is that perpetually they give mediocre customer service. They consistently and persistently neglect to do the small things that would make their customer service better and better.

Company leaders that really want to excel in customer service delivery need to instill a sense of mission in all of their providers to strive to please every customer every day. The ideal will not always be met, but at the end of the day it will be these companies that retain customers, grow market share, and make money. Keeping the *Two Factor Theory* ... in mind will help any provider to "stay on his or her toes" and be quick to do things that make customers happy.

CHAPTER 8

CUSTOMER SERVICE DIMENSION: INFORMATIONAL

A large part of the delivery of customer service concerns passing information back and forth. The provider or salesperson who is most knowledgeable, has the most *information*, usually has the best chance of being able to help the customer. Many people have heard these types of questions and comments: *Will you please put me in touch with someone who knows what is going on? I'd simply like to talk to someone who knows how to fix the problem. Is there an expert on the staff who would know what to do?*

The person having the most useful information is highly sought after because people realize that if he or she does not have the answer to a problem, that person is still the one most likely to know where to go to get the answer. The *informational dimension* of customer service events, the focus of this chapter, is checked in Text Box 8-1.

Dimensions of Customer Service Events

- Accessible
- Temporal
- Emotional
- ▶ Informational
- Aptitudinal
- Solutional
- Relational

Text Box 8-1

Information as a Conceptual Tool

Knowing the definition of a word is to possess information. A useful analogy can be drawn between tools such as one may keep in a tool box and knowing definitions of words. Tools such as screw drivers, pliers, and wrenches can help solve certain mechanical problems. A screw is loose so one tightens it with a screw driver. A nut is loose so one tightens it with a wrench. A wire needs to be cut so one does it with a pair of "*diagonals*."

In the same manner, knowing the definitions of special words can be tools that help us solve conceptual problems that often translate into solutions for practical problems. Also, possessing specialized bodies of information or clusters of information (not just single words) can function as tools that help solve more complex problems.

If one has appropriate tools in a toolbox, that person may be able to drive nails, pull nails, saw boards, drill holes, and cut wires. Such people can do many different things because they possess many different tools. It takes very little imagination to leap from physical tools to intellectual tools. The more one knows, the more bodies of special information one possesses, the greater the range of problems one can understand and, potentially, can fix.

What types of information are important for the delivery of customer service? There are three broad classes of information that are important. ***First*** is information about the needs, wants, motives, desires, and problems that the customer brings to the provider. ***Second*** is information about one's own products that could solve a customer's problems. ***Third*** is information about environmental forces such as social, educational, economic, legislative, financial, and political that may impact the world of business and may bear upon needs and problems of the customer. Knowledge about these different domains of information can function as tools to solve a customer's problems.

Customer Information

The first task of the customer service provider or salesperson is to learn what the customer is after, what will satisfy him or her, or what will resolve some problem the customer has presented. There must be some interaction. *Usually, the service provider can learn more about the needs of the customer when listening rather than talking.* The information gleaned may concern a wide range of needs and problems. A common mistake made by providers is that of being impatient; they can hardly restrain themselves; they eagerly await openings that will allow them to tell the customer what they want the customer to hear rather than to extend opportunities to the customer that allow the customer to further clarify his or her problems. If one listens, the customer will often pinpoint the help that is being sought. One does not have to figure it out; the customer figures it out for the provider. What is most important to the provider is a clear, valid understanding of the concerns, frustrations, wants, needs, and wishes of the customer. It is better to allow the customer to say these things than for the provider to assume prior knowledge about how the customer thinks and feels.

Possessing information about what is going on inside the customer is more important than possessing information about one's own products. *Why would that be?* The answer is that the first order of business for most customers is to make sure that the provider has a clear understanding of his or her problem. For the most part, customers want to hear about solutions after they have been allowed to say what is wrong.

If the provider knows clearly what is going on, what is wanted, and what will solve a customer's problem, then a solution may be proposed. Of course, the provider would like to propose a solution using his or her own company's products. If a provider lacks knowledge of his or her company's products, the needed information can be obtained from a colleague, a training video, or looked up in a book or manual. What the provider cannot do is open a book, a report, or a set of guidelines and find information about the wants, concerns, needs, and frustrations of an individual customer. Only the customer can give that information.

Main Product Information

Each customer service provider and each salesperson should understand the nature, design, qualities, features, and functions of the products (be they tangible or intangible) that his or her company sells. These products are the ostensible reasons why the customer has reached out for help, or has permitted a provider to meet with him or her to talk about needs, problems, products, and solutions.

Ideally, this information is learned before the provider has contact with the customer. It is learned through reading books and manuals, attending workshops and seminars, being trained or personally tutored, watching videos, and by having practical, hands-on experience at working with the products in question.

It's nearly impossible to deliver excellent customer service if one does not have a good grasp of the features and advantages of his or her products and does not see how their applications can meet a customer's needs. Of course, there are exceptions to everything including this idea. A provider may be so alert, courteous, friendly, attentive, and dedicated to assisting a customer that any personal insufficiency of product knowledge is forgiven or excused. Providers who are unable to personally deliver a solution for a customer's problem may still succeed in establishing such a positive relationship that the customer will return at a later time to do other business with the provider.

Business Context Information

The third class of information that is important concerns the social, community, business, educational, economic, governing, and legislative ambiences within which business transactions occur. Of course, to say that these areas of knowledge are important is not the same as to say that service providers must be deeply informed in all of these areas. But, it is worthwhile to note that providers and salespeople who possess broad understanding of societal forces that could affect a customer's business probably have an edge over other providers that do not have this knowledge. For example, a staffing company provider having some grasp of production methods, labor trends, emerging insurance requirements, pending legislation, and local human resource issues could find it easier to reason with and to find common ground with a customer that routinely employees hundred's of temporary workers than would another provider lacking this broad understanding of forces that may affect the customer's business.

Salespeople and customer service providers are wise to read widely about societal processes such as economic and legislative trends that may affect the industries that they attempt to serve. Having awareness of relevant contextual information and being able to engage the customer in such areas may enhance the image of the salesperson or the provider as an expert, but it remains that the most important information to possess and to focus upon is information about the internal motives and needs of the customer.

Making Providers Better Informed

Elwood Staffing executive leadership is committed to the idea that training should cover a broad range of content areas, should include all staff, and should be ongoing. What this means is that large bodies of *information* have been translated into training modules many of which can be accessed over the internet. All internal employees receive ongoing training over a wide range of work related content areas. Training modules are interactive, are mostly created in-house, and are constantly reviewed and updated. Assessments are built into the training modules. New modules are introduced as needed. It is the goal of Elwood Staffing that all employees learn the *Elwood Way* of doing things. Competitive advantages are created by stressing best practices.

Much training is done in face-to-face settings and other training is provided via the internet so that new training modules can be made immediately available to all employees in every field location. Records of staff participation in the training program are maintained. Continuous training is stressed so that each person shall possess all needed *information* that would enable him or her to provide *Superior Customer Service* to all customers whether they are *external, internal, primary, or secondary customers.*

CHAPTER 9

CUSTOMER SERVICE DIMENSION: APTITUDINAL

The word aptitude has many uses, but is mostly defined as inherent talent to learn. As used in this book, aptitude is meant to cover inherent or natural talent to learn plus those skills and abilities that have been acquired through practice, training, and education. One may speak of a person who has good aptitude to learn to play musical instruments. Another person may have great aptitude for grasping mathematical concepts. Good students have strong aptitudes for learning academic subject matter. Regarding customer service events, one thinks of the *aptitudinal dimension* as referring to the full range of talents, mental prowess, know-how, skills, and cognitive abilities that a provider may bring to bear to meet the needs and to solve the problems of a customer.

Dimensions of Customer Service Events
Accessible
Temporal
Emotional
Informational
► Aptitudinal
Solutional
Relational

Text Box 9-1

Providers having the greatest aptitudes are the providers most likely to deliver good customer service. They know the answers to give. They know where to find helpful information that may not be at their finger tips. They listen and absorb. They grasp what it is that the customer is attempting to explain. They sense how he or she feels. They have a knack for saying the right things. They see how to put disjointed facts together to find solutions for problems. They are able to convey to the customer that they see the difficulties and challenges confronting the customer and, furthermore, that they understand things well enough that they can propose workable solutions. They project competency. Aptitude means skill. Skillful providers know how to bring the loose ends of a customer service experience together into a meaningful whole that results in a satisfied customer. As shown in Text Box 9-1, attention is now focused upon the *aptitudinal dimension* of customer service.

General Cognitive Ability

One of the most clearly established relationships in the field of applied psychology is that at all levels of work, from custodians to presidents, those of greater cognitive ability are more productive than those of lesser ability (Hunter & Hunter, 1984; Schmidt & Hunter, 1998). *Why should this be? Why should those of greater general cognitive ability get more done than those having lesser ability?* There are at least three explanations for this relationship.

First, people of greater ability have less need for supervisory guidance and explanation than people of lesser ability. They understand the immediate task. They can take the ball and run with it. While a supervisor is explaining a task to a person of lesser ability, the person of greater ability is already performing the task. ***Second***, people of greater ability see end goals and their work task implications more quickly than people of lesser ability. They see the big picture. When they see reasonable actions that would move an entire project further along, they take those actions. During such times, less able workers may be awaiting explanations and leadership from superiors. ***Third***, people of greater ability have more confidence and imagination than their coworkers about how to do things. Even if they do not know how to do something, they feel that if they apply themselves they will learn how to do it and will get the job done.

If it is true that people of greater ability are more productive than people of lesser ability, is there any reason to expect things to be different in the customer service arena? Author Dave Elwood's answer is "*No.*" All other things being equal, the brightest people will give the best customer service. Sewell & Brown (2002) expressed a similar sentiment: "*We try to hire only smart people who understand how we do things. Those kinds of people will be more productive and go out of their way to provide excellent customer service …*"

Assessing Aptitude

Aptitude assessment is a huge field. There are literally thousands of published mental ability tests that meet varying standards of scientific credibility. Many of these tests are relevant to the delivery of customer service. However, it would be impractical to measure all dimensions of aptitude that could be relevant to customer service.

If one has the option of acquiring and using ability tests to help in selecting customer service providers, what instruments should he or she select? Answer: Seek a reasonably good measure of *general cognitive ability*. If possible, select a procedure or procedures that include measures of verbal ability and mathematical ability. The reason these two measures are important is that they correlate more highly than do other measures of cognitive skill with *overall cognitive ability.*

At Elwood Staffing, potential candidates for internal positions are asked to take tests that help gauge their general cognitive ability levels. Significant weight is given to test results, but they represent only one factor in hiring decisions. Many cognitive ability tests are available commercially and are reasonably priced. They are relatively easy to administer and score, do not require professional certification (e.g., licensure as a psychologist) for use, and may require less than an hour of time for the applicant and the staff person who handles the tests. Any test selected should include information about normative samples and should provide *centile* scores (often called "*percentile*" scores) that help the test user to know how the subject scored on a scale from 1 to 99 compared to normative samples.

It is desirable to have a trained professional available, at least on a periodic consultative basis, to help make sure test material is handled properly, that standardized procedures for administering and scoring tests are followed, and that the meanings and conclusions drawn from test findings are appropriate and uniform.

As a cautionary note, it is easy for people who are not fully trained and licensed professionals to develop manners and methods of administering, scoring, and reporting test findings that do not meet minimum professional standards that should be adhered to in testing situations. In one such case that author Dave Elwood is aware of a person helping collect testing data completely ignored strict time standards for administering the tests. When the testing data were reviewed, they were noted to be so much out of line with normal expectancies that the person handling the tests was questioned and openly admitted that no attention was paid to timing standards. In that case, the test results were declared totally invalid and were discarded. When problems such as these occur in the use of tests, they are likely to be the result of inadequate supervision and training.

In summary, the use of tests can help one select applicants most likely to provide outstanding customer service, but staff members handling test materials should have proper training and supervision in how to handle and to administer tests.

Vocational Interest Patterns

Vocational interest patterns are not usually thought of as aptitudes, but there is a sense in which they are similar to aptitudes. That is, people who have certain vocational interest patterns often find it easier to learn to do jobs that correlate highly with their vocational interest structures than do other people having totally different vocational interest structures. In these cases, patterns of vocational interests function similarly to aptitudes.

It is a little bit like swimming upstream or downstream. If one is in a line of work that correlates with his or her vocational interest structure, then that person is swimming downstream. Everything seems easy and fits into place. But, if vocational interest patterns are markedly at odds with the person's actual line of work, if there is no commonality between what one feels inclined to do versus what one is required to do, then that person may be swimming upstream. That person is always trying to overcome things just to stay even. The responses that person must make have limited natural or intuitive feel to them.

According to psychologist John Holland (Holland, 1994; Holland, Fritzsche, & Powell, 1997), vocational interest patterns for specific occupations can be efficiently described as clustering around six major themes: *Realistic, Investigative, Artistic, Social, Enterprising, and Conventional.*

The theme of greatest interest to people in business and commerce is the *enterprising theme*. People whose likes, dislikes, and preferences focus around the enterprising theme are often described as *leaders*. They enjoy being in business, like buying and selling, like to deal with the public, and like associating with people having status.

Some may argue: *Aren't those things true for many people?* The answer is: *To a degree, but not so strongly as for the enterprising types.* For example, people whose likes, preferences, and skills align closely with the *investigative theme* tend to be more highly motivated by science, math, discovery, and scientific theories rather than making money which is a major motive of the enterprising theme.

Elwood Staffing hired a man who was well-liked, but he did not stay long. He quit saying he was not "*cut out*" to work behind a desk. He started his own remodeling and repair business. Had he completed a vocational interest survey, he likely would have scored high on the *realistic* theme—liking to work with one's hands, being out of doors, and using equipment and machinery.

A young woman fresh out of college expressed a strong desire to work for Elwood Staffing. She was bright, had an excellent academic record, came with high recommendations, and was a person of good character. Her summer work experience was with non-profit organizations and her extracurricular activities were focused on helping needy people.

After working for about three months, she submitted her letter of resignation saying she felt the staffing business was not a "*good fit*" for her. She thanked Elwood Staffing for the opportunity that had been given to her and explained that she planned to start working as a "*substitute teacher.*" Had she completed a vocational interest survey, she likely would have scored high on the *social theme.* Those who score high on the *social theme* are often called *helpers.* They like to assist, nurture, facilitate, and volunteer. They represent occupations such as teachers, social workers, welfare workers, religious workers, and volunteer workers.

So, if a company is to provide the best customer service, people are needed who have the ability, the vocational inclination, and the experience to focus on the customer and who are happier doing this than doing anything else. Whether or not tests are used to evaluate vocational interest patterns, one should attempt to select people who are drawn to, interested in, and approving of *enterprising* motives (e.g., making a profit), activities, and goals. These are the people who are most likely to see the importance of winning customers, keeping customers, making them happy, and delivering *Superior Customer Service.*

Specialized Skills

Since author Dave Elwood has so strongly stressed the importance of hiring the brightest people whenever possible, one may ask *What then is the place in the world of work for people of normal-average cognitive skills?* Answer: There are millions upon millions of jobs across all industries that are specialized and that require intensive training to master, but can be handled fully capably by ordinary people of average ability. The people needed for these positions are mature, conscientious, willing to learn, motivated to do a good job, and more focused on job security than on promotions. Such people often provide *extraordinary customer service* and in the process discover they were not so ordinary after all.

Importance of Experience

Another cautionary thought may be in order regarding the matter of trying to hire people having high aptitudes—no matter how much aptitude, or mental ability, a person may have, either because of natural talent or intensive training, experience is still needed.There is no substitute for on the job experience. Each person needs the corrective influence of experience to help him or her discern between how much was known and how much was thought to be known but was not known at all. And, one needs experience to shed light on whether or not an embraced theory has any practical usefulness. All of these things are true for the customer service field. The ideas that people hold about how to provide customer service must be validated over and over. As one goes through such processes, his or her ideas are sifted, sorted, modified, and refined. Sometimes they are contracted and sometimes expanded. Sometimes they are discarded altogether. The central point is that having great aptitude alone does not guarantee that one will deliver *Superior Customer Service.* Aptitude and experience together are the best predictors of success.

CHAPTER 10

CUSTOMER SERVICE DIMENSION: SOLUTIONAL

The *solutional dimension* of customer service events, checked in Text Box 10-1, comes into play when a customer decides that he or she has a problem, often with a *primary product*, and contacts the provider to fix the problem, to find a solution. The customer may politely request a solution, or may demand a solution. Whether or not the *solutional dimension* is relevant in a particular provider-customer interaction depends upon how the customer sees things. How customers feel about this dimension varies greatly.

Dimensions of Customer Service Events

Accessible
Temporal
Emotional
Informational
Aptitudinal
▶ Solutional
Relational

Text Box 10 1

One customer may come in "*mad as a wet hornet*" because of some perceived malfunction in a product, or because the product did not meet his expectancies. He wants it fixed, wants it fixed "*right now*," wants it replaced with a new unit, wants to exchange it for something totally different, or he may not know what he wants except to vent his anger toward the provider.

Another customer may come in with the same perceived malfunction and have a breezy, relaxed attitude about the problem and the schedule as to when he could expect the product to be fixed or replaced and ready to be taken back home. The second customer may seem more interested in browsing in the store and having a friendly chat with the provider than seeing a solution for his problem. It's up to the provider to gauge, as best he can, the priority the customer puts on finding a solution for a problem. If it's an urgent matter to the customer, it should be an urgent matter to the provider. Even if the customer seems calm about the problem, the provider should take any complaint seriously and work as quickly as he can to find a solution.

The underlying reason why a customer demands something be fixed or taken care of is sometimes unknown. If there is an obvious defect or malfunction in a *primary product*, that problem may be the easiest one to fix. A repair can be made, or the customer can be given a new product. In many cases, these steps can be taken quickly and they represent the most economical solutions.

If there has been a failure in the *customer service product* such as a provider having been rude or insensitive, then more time and patience may be required to find a solution, or "*to fix the problem.*" For certain, if a customer is deeply upset, it is more important to try to help settle the customer's emotions before attempting to fix something that may be broken.

Scope and Nature of Dissatisfaction Problems

Customer dissatisfaction with some aspect of business transactions ranges from barely discernable feelings of disappointment to extreme anger. Fortunately, extreme anger is seldom seen. Most customers are pleased with the *main products* they buy. *Disappointments are much more likely to be with* ***customer service components*** *of business* *transactions than with* ***main products.*** For example, the *Enterprise* car rental company kept records for years about the reasons customers stopped doing business with them. They found that 68 percent of customers stopped because of the "*poor way they were treated by employees of the company*" while only 14 percent stopped because of the main product—the rental cars (Kazanjian, 2007). As one knows from the *Two Factor Theory of Customer Service*, the rental car was the *main product*, or the *primary product,* and how *Enterprise* employees treated customers was the *customer service product.* In these data, the *main product* was much better approved of than was the *customer service product.*

When a customer goes so far as to register a complaint with a store or with a provider, what is the likely basis for the complaint? Will it be the ***primary product*** *or the* ***customer service product****?* The *Enterprise* data just presented suggest that many more complaints will be made about *customer service products* than about *main products*—in fact, customer service complaints should be almost five times as great as main product complaints. *But is that the true reality?*

The probable reality is that customers are more likely to make verbal complaints to store owners or to providers about *main product failures* than to voice complaints about *customer service failures. If this is so, why would it be so?* There are at least five reasons why customers may be *unwilling to speak up* when customer service failures occur: 1) reluctance to say things that could cause a provider to feel bad, 2) reluctance to say something that could cause a provider to lose his or her job, 3) reluctance to say something that could make the customer himself or herself appear to be thin skinned or fussy, 4) belief that providing good customer service is the job of the provider or store owner—not something the customer should have to bother with, or 5) belief that a complaint would make no difference, so why bother to make it.

Anecdotal types of examples may shed light on why customers don't like to complain about customer service failures (unless the failure was extremely egregious): A customer may go to a **Customer Service Desk** in a store and return a toaster because the heating element burned out the first time the toaster was used. The customer wants a new toaster. The toaster was a *main product*. But, how often does one hear of a customer going to a **Customer Service Desk,** or to any other part of a store, or to any person in a store to report: *When I was in the store yesterday a lady wearing a pretty blue and white dress served me. She showed me some skirts. She was nice enough, but she seemed so aloof and distant that I came away from interacting with her feeling down emotionally (**low** on the **emotional dimension** of customer service events,) and I just wanted to share my experience with you as manager of the store.* Such a complaint could occur, but it would be exceedingly rare compared to complaints about primary product failures. What would make such a complaint even rarer still would be for the customer to add that the saleslady should be fired so that the customer would not have to interact with her again or that, at least, the saleslady should be referred for psychotherapy. Customer complaints such as these would likely be seen as overly presumptuous and deserving rejection.

It should be noted that it is one thing for a customer to avoid going through the formal process of re-visiting a store or re-contacting a provider to verbally complain about an incident of poor customer service, and a quite different thing for the same customer to talk freely and openly with family, friends, and, perhaps, even strangers about the very same incident of poor customer service. For example, a customer with an engineering background could go to a home improvement store looking for a special wrench and have the misfortune of being served by a salesperson that could not help her and who barely knew the difference between an *allen wrench* and a *phillips screwdriver* (***low*** on the *aptitudinal dimension*). The customer could assume that the store manager was aware of the skill level of the salesperson and could avoid making a complaint, but that would not stop her from talking openly to family and friends about how limited and how un-helpful the store salesperson was.

The *solutional dimension* comes into play when customers decide that a problem is present that needs to be fixed by the provider. Whether the basis for the problem is the *primary product* or the *customer service product* and whether the customer is calm or emotionally upset, when a customer asks for help, the provider needs to "*pull all stops*" and work as hard as he or she can to solve the problem, to find a solution, and to restore the customer's feelings to those of satisfaction. In the following sections, some problem solving strategies and approaches will be reviewed.

Service Recovery: On the Spot Solutions

The phrase "*Service Recovery*," often found in customer service literature, refers to customers requesting or demanding that problems be addressed. All, or almost all, problems that would be included in *service recovery* would also be included as *solutional dimension* problems. Berry (1995) listed five guidelines that could help in service recovery situations. In paraphrased form, the guidelines were 1) offer a personalized apology to the customer, 2) attempt to resolve the customer's problem as quickly as possible, 3) attempt to resolve the problem at the point of contact, if possible, 4) keep the customer informed about what you are doing to help him, and 5) work to create a "fair solution" to the problem. Providers should know the limits of their skills to solve problems, but as much as possible the first provider should attempt to shepherd the customer through the problem solving process. Research performed at FedEx showed that if a customer had to deal with only one provider to resolve his problem 77 percent felt the service was OK, but if a second provider was required then only 61 percent felt the service was OK (Berry, 1995).

LeBoeuf (1987) offered wise counsel about finding solutions to a customer's problems. He advised that a provider should 1) *keep cool*—even if a customer may be showing strong negative emotions, 2) *be empathetic*—let the customer know you understand how he feels, 3) *take action to solve the problem*—the customer needs more than just understanding, 4) bring the incident to a polite close, and 5) *recognize you can't win them all.* LeBoeuf's fifth point—*you can't win them all*—is practical and realistic, but it's also important to keep in mind that there may be times when a provider should go all out, be willing to take "*heroic*" steps, to solve a customer's problem (Bly, 1993). When service failures occur, the customer has been inconvenienced and may also have lost some confidence in the provider. Carr (1990) advised that the provider needs to do more than just restore service to the pre-failure level. He needs, as much as possible, to create added value for the customer to make up for previous inconvenience.

Brinkman & Kirschner (2006) discussed several techniques for trying to help customers who are emotionally upset or angry. Always be polite. *Deal with the customer's emotions before trying to solve his other problems.* Let the customer know you are listening. Project a caring attitude. Take ownership of the problem the customer brings to you. Keep careful records of the things said by the customer in describing his problem. Keep the customer informed about what you are doing to help—communicate. Ask questions to get a clearer picture of the customer's problem. Ask the customer for feedback about the effectiveness of the thing you have done to help him.

Enterprise has become America's "*number one*" car rental company, and much of the credit for its ascent to the top is tied to how Enterprise people look at and treat customers. Kazanjian (2007), in his book on Enterprise titled *Exceeding Customer Expectations*, pointed out that "*unsatisfied customers*" were actively sought out at Enterprise with the goal of making them into "*loyal fans.*" He went ahead to list "*eight steps*" that Enterprise employees were taught to take to turn "*an* ***angry*** *customer around.*" In essence the steps were: 1) actively listen and understand, 2) record what customer says, 3) apologize, 4) learn what customer wants, 5) propose a solution, 6) if customer rejects the solution, ask him/her to propose a solution, 7) make follow-up phone call, and 8) never let customer lose face.

Each technique outlined above has value for dealing with customers' "on the spot" demands for solutions to problems. The particular combination of techniques that would be most helpful will vary from one industry to another. However, some techniques are almost always appropriate and helpful: 1) apologize, 2) be empathetic, 3)stay calm, 4) be caring, 5) listen carefully, 6) start the search for a solution as quickly as possible, 7) communicate—tell customer what you are doing to help him, and 8) never let customer lose face.

Complainers Create Opportunities

Research reported by the *U.S. Office of Consumer Affairs* showed that most customers that had complaints did not bother to report them, but for those that did complain and had their problems handled well, 50 to 80 percent said they were likely to do further business with that same company, but for customers who had complaints but said nothing, only 9 to 37 percent would likely do further business with that company (Timm, 2001). One lesson in these findings is that if one can get a customer to complain, he has a better chance of retaining his business than if the customer never complains.

Timm outlined several steps that providers can take that will improve their chances of dealing successfully with complaints. *Make it easy for customers to complain*—if customers must fill out forms, make many phone calls to get to the right person, or write a formal letter of complaint, they are less likely to complain—the access barriers are too high. *Act quickly to solve the problem*—show empathy for customer and immediately begin the search for a solution. *Take substantial steps to make-up for inconvenience*—work not only to restore service but also do extra things to convey to customer that you are sorry for the fact that a problem even occurred. *Try to put systems into place that will catch complaints before they happen—"cut them off at the pass"*—after a provider has had some experience, the times, places, and circumstances that produce complaints will become better known: be ready to deal with complaints before they emerge. *Don't challenge the customer*—nothing is gained by arguing with a customer. As a final note, the *Office of Consumer Affairs* found that customers that had complaints but did not report them were, nevertheless, quite willing to talk about them with other people. In fact, the average non-complaining, dissatisfied customer shared his unhappy experiences with 12 other people.

Grow Service by Anticipating Service Failures

Kaufman (2012) made the point that no matter how well prepared a provider or a company may be, problems will come. Service failures will happen. There will be surprises. But, these things are not reasons to avoid planning for how to handle problems that are bound to come up in the future in the normal course of business. Kaufman outlined six broad strategies for anticipating and attempting to handle service failures.

One*, get senior management support*—make the point that mistakes will occur, that problem solvers need management support, and that program development to handle mistakes may cost money. ***Two***, *practice your recovery plan*—imagine what could go wrong, rather than to wait until a problem "pops up," and organize SWAT-like teams that go through drills to handle most likely problems. ***Three****, go hunting for service problems*—be aggressive, put the spotlight on flaws in the service delivery system. ***Four****, empower frontline staff*—enable service personnel, give them authority to handle problems right on the spot. ***Five****, go for the big win-win*—don't just fix problems, go all out to *delight* the customer. ***Six****, lock in the gains*—collect great stories of customer service, give special recognition to outstanding providers, create an honor roll for providers.

Going More Than Halfway: Going all the Way

If there's a gold standard, a platinum standard, or any other ultra-high standard respecting how to look at customers, treat customers, and handle warrantees, guarantees, returns, and complaints, it is probably embedded in the philosophy and life of the late Sam Walton, founder of *Walmart*. Some facts about *Walmart*: 11,000 stores in 27 countries, 2.2 million associates, world's largest private employer, world's largest retailer, and 2013 annual sales of $466 billion.

Given the staggering size of Walmart and the enormous vision of "Mr. Sam," it is no surprise that his thinking about the importance of customers would also be grand. Michael Bergdahl (2006), *Director of Home Office People* for Walmart, worked closely with Mr. Sam. In his book on Walton, *The Ten Rules of Sam Walton*, Bergdahl shared a detailed picture of Mr. Sam's ideas about customers.

Paraphrased: Exceed the customer's expectations. The customer is the most important person in our business. We are completely dependent on the customer. Customers do us a favor to shop in our stores. Customers are insiders. We don't argue with customers. Customers are not statistics, they are people. Give the most courteous and attentive service to the customer that you possibly can. The people who buy our products pay our salaries. The customer is the boss. Customers are the lifeblood of our company.

Mr. Sam's ideas about customers were not idle slogans. They were taught, stressed, repeated, and lived out by Mr. Sam, the managers, directors, and all other company leaders who came under his influence and saw the example of his life.

So, to consider the ***solutional dimension****, the focus of this chapter, how is a complaining, demanding, sometimes hostile, customer,* ***someone who wants a solution right now****, served within the Walmart system?*

The answer to this question can be found in two interviews Bergdahl conducted with *Walmart* store managers. The first interview was with a retired store manager who had worked directly with Mr. Sam. The manager stated: "*He said it doesn't matter whether you have a receipt or not, it doesn't matter when you bought it, it doesn't matter whether anything is wrong with it or not, if you don't like it and you don't want it any more, you bring it back and we will give you your money back with a smile.*"

In the second interview, a different store manager said this about Mr. Sam and the company's "*satisfaction guaranteed*" standard: "*He said that if the customer buys a lawn mower and they use it for three years and they drag it back into the store with the wheels falling off and otherwise falling apart and they ask to return it, don't question them about why they returned it! He said just take care of the customer. .... Always remember to take care of the customer because 97 percent of your customers are good, honest, hardworking people and maybe 3 percent are dishonest.*"

For those providers seeking solutions for a customer's problems and who feel that clues as to where to find those solutions could be embedded in the philosophy and practices of Walmart, the message is clear: ***Take care of the customer. Help the customer. Accept the***

customer. Understand the customer. Appreciate the customer. Treat the customer like a member of one's family. Always do anything and everything that one can to take care of the customer. Keep the customer happy so that he will keep coming back again and again.

Each provider and each company has a different set of needs concerning matters of service recovery and customer dissatisfaction. A program of *Superior Customer Service* and a program of "*service recovery*" that works wonderfully well for a small retailer whose top dollar item is under five hundred dollars might not work at all for a car dealership that sells new cars with average price tags over sixty thousand dollars. The leaders of each company must decide through experience and wise judgment what *Superior Customer Service* and service recovery looks like for them. But, size, either large or small, should not stop a company from striving to offer truly outstanding customer service.

CHAPTER 11

CUSTOMER SERVICE DIMENSION: RELATIONAL

The *relational dimension* of customer service, noted in Text Box 11-1, implies being personable, warm, caring, friendly, and focused upon the customer's needs. The customer comes quickly to understand that the provider sees him or her as important, worthy of time, and valuable whether or not a purchase is made. The relational dimension is interpersonal. As feelings of confidence, trust, and acceptance start emerging, this aspect of customer service becomes increasingly important. Those providers who are most successful at inspiring these types of feelings in customers will have the best chances of making sales and earning customers' loyalties.

Dimensions of Customer Service Events

- Accessible
- Temporal
- Emotional
- Informational
- Aptitudinal
- Solutional
- ▶ Relational

Text Box 11-1

This dimension of customer service builds upon dimensions of customer service discussed earlier. Easy accessibility of service, promptness of service, and service that stirs positive emotions usually point toward good customer service and help pave the way for positive relationships to emerge. However, some customers may actively oppose developing close personal relationships with providers. Bell (1996) wisely pointed out that some customers have no interest in developing a "*partnership*" (read as "*relationship*") with providers. As soon as familiarity and friendliness emerge they start looking for a new provider. These customers want nothing more than simple, direct, straight-to-the-point service and may become annoyed or impatient if they sense the provider is working too hard to build a friendship or to offer help the customer is not looking for and does not welcome.

There are few things in life that author Dave Elwood's wife has enjoyed more than doing things for our grandchildren. One very satisfying activity was to take our three-year-old grandson to pre-school one day a week. On one such occasion, she picked him up from his home, buckled him into a car seat, and off they went. Soon after they got underway, he said, "*I don't like you and I don't like your car.*" This "*put-down*" was followed a little later by "*I don't want to talk to you and I don't want you to talk to me.*" She took his rejections in stride, tried to engage him, and concluded his rejection of her was based on jealousy stemming from attention she had been giving to his new three-month-old brother. After about a week had passed and she had done some favors for him, he accepted her again. Sometimes it happens that way with customers. A customer may seem aloof, indifferent, or even negative toward friendly gestures regardless of how appropriately and fittingly they are extended, but if the customer (or potential customer) and his or her *need for space* are respected and friendly gestures are not forced, the customer may later come around and allow a true friendship to emerge.

Spontaneous Reactions

Spontaneous reactions are basic to human social interaction and they play an important role in development of positive relationships between providers and customers. These reactions are called spontaneous, but they were embedded in and grew out of long histories of social experience and maturation before they become spontaneous. Once they are established, almost every person can perform them with very little practice. For example, if a supervisor says "*smile*" at each person who enters the door, that response can be made easily without practice although at first it could seem awkward and uncomfortable for some people.

Spontaneous reactions also include such simple acts as *looking at a person* and *greeting the person*. These responses are not difficult to make, but it is sometimes true that people who fill critical "*first contact*" roles fail to look, smile, and to greet. At least they fail to do them in timely fashions. A person who worked in the Elwood Staffing front office, in early years of the company, was a quite good employee, but when she performed transcription she would not allow anyone or anything to interrupt her typing. The typing could have waited. Looking at, smiling at, and greeting visitors should have taken priority.

Aspects of posture are important in establishing positive relationships with customers. They are not automatic, but they can become spontaneous with a little practice. Providers should orient themselves toward the customer when they greet him or her. To do so is to convey to the customer that the provider notices the customer, recognizes the customer's importance, and is focused upon the customer. Torso position is important. To be stooped over a keyboard or to be slouched in one's chair when greeting a customer or visitor sets a less than ideal professional tone for the balance of the person's visit.

Some short and simple verbal responses come close to fitting into the category of spontaneous reactions. When a visitor or customer appears, the *first contact* person should always say something such as:

Hi, how may I help you? Hello, how may I help you? Hello, my name is Sarah. May I help you? What is appropriate will vary from situation to situation and from person to person. The main point is that the provider should initiate contact when a customer appears and should offer assistance when doing so would be appropriate.

When dealing with a customer, the simple words *Please, Thank you*, and *May I* should be used often. They are rarely overused. Most people can think of times when they were annoyed or put off because a provider was indifferent or gave them brusque treatment, but ***very few*** people can recall times when they were annoyed or angered because a provider went overboard in saying *Please, Thank you*, and *May I.* At some point during contact with a customer, it is appropriate for the provider to say something such as *Thank you for coming to our office. We are pleased to see you. Please come back again. Thanks for your business.* Whatever specific comments are used, a provider should express appreciation to the customer or potential customer for having come toward the provider (Willingham, 1992).

Strategic Responses

The phrase *strategic responses,* as used in the *Two Factor Theory of Customer Service,* refers to responses that are usually complex, require some rehearsal, and may be challenging to execute. Examples of strategic responses are *projecting a positive attitude, appearing confident,* and *presenting oneself as a person who is comfortable and relaxed.* One knows that people who respond in these ways are usually more attractive interpersonally than people who appear negative, fearful, irritated, or ill at ease. Typically, one would rather spend time with people who are positive and confident than to spend time with people who are negative and uncomfortable. *Would it not also follow that providers who project positive attitudes, exude confidence, and appear comfortable and relaxed have greater chances of establishing positive, lasting relationships with customers than other providers coming across as negative, ill at ease, and tense?* The answer is "*Yes*."

Other examples of *strategic responses* are *remembering the names of customers, allowing the customer to talk more than requiring the customer to listen, speaking clearly and distinctly, and using good grammar.* None of these things alone will create a positive relationship with a customer, but each one helps. Dressing appropriately for one's business role is also important. Formal business attire is not mandatory in all situations, but it's rarely a mistake to show up in one's "*Sunday best*." Dressing appropriately not only makes a good impression for the provider and his or her company, it also conveys honor and respect to the people being served. Such providers feel the customers they serve are important enough that they are willing to go to the trouble of dressing up for them.

Few things are more important to customers than for providers to show genuine interest in them. This point is difficult to over emphasize. LeBoeuf (1987) beautifully illustrated the point in a story about two ladies having lunch. They talked about why one of the ladies, Jane, chose NOT to marry "Bob" and married "Bill" instead.

Jane explained: "*Bob is Mr. Everything. He's handsome, well-educated, extremely intelligent, clever, and has a very successful career. In fact, when I was with Bob I felt like I was with the most wonderful person in the world*." Her friend then asked, "*Well, since Bob seemed so wonderful, why did you reject him and marry Bill instead?*" Jane answered: "*When I'm with Bill, I feel like* ***I'm*** *the most wonderful person in the world*." How true it is that we most enjoy relationships with people who have a knack for helping us think well of ourselves.

It is easy to be glib when talking about *strategic responses*. One may be fully persuaded that certain responses are desirable and that they would probably help in business, but giving mental assent to the desirability of certain responses is much different from being able smoothly to execute such responses. Many things are easier said than done. For example, the person who is absolutely terrified at giving a speech in public is probably helped very little by someone saying to him "*act confident.*" Nevertheless, one is wise to talk about things that are desirable to do even if they may difficult to do. The first step is to talk about desirable behavior. The next step is to get started doing things that have a chance of creating desirable behavior.

Providers who excel in the art of establishing relationships have mastered a battery of words, phrases, comments, questions, and observations designed to "*draw people out*" and to set the stage for a degree of friendly contact. For some providers, the inventory of verbal skills they have in this area are so thoroughly practiced and integrated into their personalities that they seem "*second nature.*"

For providers who feel they are not very good at building relationships, one of the most helpful things to do is to break complex skills down into smaller parts. Each person reading these words has the capacity to do this. After breaking complex tasks down into smaller components, practice the performance of each component to perfection, and then recombine all components into the masterful delivery of one complex well-integrated response. To a degree, this is comparable to committing a long poem to memory. At the start, one does not even know the first line of the poem; after intensive practice, he is able to recite a ten verse poem from beginning to end flawlessly. Those who can create, perfect, and deliver what I have called *strategic responses* increase their chances to establish positive relationships with customers.

Personality and Character

Personality and character influence the types of relationships that emerge between providers and customers the same as *spontaneous reactions* and *strategic responses* influence these relationships. But there is an important difference. *Spontaneous reactions* and their more complex cousins, *strategic responses,* may be modified through deliberate programs of practice. It is much harder to do the same thing with traits of personality and character. They are deeply rooted and ingrained in one's psychological and biological makeup.

Traits of personality and character that are important for establishing stable, positive relationships between providers and customers are: trust, honesty, integrity, reliability, openness, respect, compassion, generosity, persistence, commitment, discipline, friendliness, and a positive attitude. This list is not comprehensive. Literally thousands of terms have been used to describe nuances of personality and character.

A provider whose main personality patterns would be described as open, friendly, generous, respectful of others, and positive would be expected to develop better relationships with customers than other providers who would not possess these or similar traits. A provider who would be described as aloof, introverted, irritable, suspicious, and unfriendly would have a far lesser chance of establishing close, positive relations with customers.

What conclusions should one draw from these observations about personality and character? The main conclusions are: ***One***, a*ttempt* ***up front*** *to select providers having the personality qualities and traits of character that one feels are important for establishing positive, stable relations with customers.* ***Two,*** *use training programs to modify* ***spontaneous reactions*** *and* ***strategic responses. Three***, *lean away from trying to use training programs to modify personality and character.*

Mitchells/Richards Clothing Stores

A good example of the importance of the relationship dimension of customer service is found in the *Mitchells/Richards Company.*

Mitchells/Richards sell suits and dresses, one at a time, to individual customers. They have only two stores, one in Westport, Connecticut with population of 28,000 and one in Greenwich with population of about 60,000. It is a family owned and operated business.

There's nothing unique about family owned stores that sell clothing in moderate sized towns. But, there is a unique and stunning fact about *Mitchells/Richards* that will grab the attention of most business owners. In 2002 their annual sales were more than $65 million. *How could two retail clothing stores located in two relatively small towns, not New York and Paris mind you, have combined sales over $65 million in one year?* Jack Mitchell (2003), CEO of *Mitchells/ Richards*, answers this question in his fascinating book *Hug Your Customers.*

Mitchell and his entire staff are strongly focused upon the customer. They are people oriented. Mitchell's personal devotion to the customer is illustrated through a story he told about his participation as a panelist in a conference attended by chief executive officers in the apparel industry. He said the conference was held in Carefree, Arizona but many of the attendees were not feeling carefree. They were struggling against competition from discount stores and dot com companies, and customers were complaining that customer service was "*dismal.*" He summed up the mood of the conference as "*somber,*" but he said his mood was not somber.

Mitchell described himself as typically ebullient. He went ahead to say "*Glasses are never half empty to my eye; they're five-eighths full. Many times they're full or overflowing.*" One of the keynote speakers at the conference talked about the decline in customer service and expressed doubt that anyone of the hundreds of executives attending the conference knew his top one hundred customers. He asked for a show of hands. Mitchell raised his hand and then was a little embarrassed to notice that his hand was the only one that had been raised. But, he said his main reaction was to be taken aback that people did not know such basic information about their businesses.

When it came Mitchell's turn to speak as a panelist, he stated, "*I know my top one thousand customers.*" He continued to say that at his company "*...everyone from the sales associate to the tailor to the delivery person concentrated on the customer ...*" All the way from a friendly greeting and a smile when they first meet to the showering of attention during the selling process, Mitchell and his associates concentrate on the customer.

When some people are bored, they may read a book. When Mitchell is bored, he often goes to his computer, pulls up the data base of his customers, punches in parameters, and pulls up his top one hundred or top one thousand customers. He studies characteristics of his customers the same as someone else might study the meanings of vocabulary words as preparation for taking the Scholastic Aptitude Test.

If $65 million in sales in one year does not make it clear that Mitchell's brand of focusing upon the customer is effective, then, think of these additional statistics: about two dozen sales associates write over $1 million of business a year; five associates write more than $2 million a year; and one associate writes over $3 million a year. Mitchell has records of his customers' purchases year after year. Some spend $5,000, some $20,000, and some spend $100,000. A few even spend $250,000 a year (that's not a typo!) in his stores. Lest one loses sight of this one salient fact, keep in mind that these numbers refer to *one customer at a time buying one suit at a time or one dress at a time for his or her personal wardrobe.*

As a concluding thought, one cannot maintain the level of business that is maintained by Jack Mitchell without establishing some enduring *relationships* with customers.

Sewell Village Cadillac

Another excellent example of the importance of the *relational* dimension of customer service is found in Sewell & Brown's (2002) account of how Carl Sewell, owner of the highly successful *Sewell Village Cadillac* auto dealership chain in Dallas, grew his company from sales of $10 million in 1968 to sales of $850 million in 2002. From the beginning, Sewell stressed the importance of one's *relationship* with the customer. Also, he required all people in the company to be involved in delivering excellent customer service. He stated "*I don't believe you can run an above average business with average employees.*" He continued to say "*We probably need to interview twenty-five people to find a really good person, and we might have to interview a hundred folks to find someone who is truly exceptional.*" As an example of a "*truly exceptional*" person, a "*Service Superstar,*" he told about his top salesperson whose dedication to pleasing the customer was so great that he sold 500 cars a year in multiple years and in one year sold more than 700 cars. Sewell commented, "*There wasn't anything he wouldn't do for a customer.*"

Another "*Service Superstar*" described by Sewell was a service manager who had "*more true empathy for customers than anyone I have ever seen.*" This service manager would meet with customers after hours, on Sunday, and would even make "*house calls*" to take care of his customers. He received more complimentary letters from customers than did all seven other service managers combined. Stories such as these suggested *strong positive interpersonal relationships* had been established between these providers and their customers.

Despite Sewell's strong emphasis on delivering excellent customer service directly to the customer, some people were critical of his way of doing things. He confessed to being "*stung*" by their comments. Most people agreed with the ways he did things, but some asserted that his approach to customers was "*all too touchy-feely,*" that he was "*wasting money by spoiling customers,*" and that his success "*stemmed from some kind of luck.*" Sewell responded to these criticisms by hiring *J. D. Power and Associates* to evaluate his company. They surveyed his customers without disclosing who had hired them to do the work.

In Sewell's own words, the results of the survey were "*gratifying.*" The percent of his customers rating "*Courtesy extended to customers*" as excellent was ***54% higher*** than for the Cadillac dealer national average. The percent rating the "*Ease of obtaining appointment(s)*" as excellent was ***39% higher*** than the national average, the percent rating "*Helpfulness of service personnel*" as excellent was ***53% higher*** than the national average, and the percent rating "*Knowledge of service personnel*" as excellent was ***57% higher*** than the national average.

Furthermore, the percent of Sewell customers stating that they were very satisfied with their cars was ***25% higher*** than the national average for Cadillac dealers. The cars were the same from dealer to dealer since they were all Cadillac dealers, but Sewell's customers were more satisfied. His explanation of the data: "*Our customers thought more of the car because of the way we treated them before and after the sale.*" Finally, the survey data showed that the percentage of Sewell customers saying they "*Definitely would*" purchase the same make of car again was ***12% higher*** than the national average for Cadillac dealers.

Sewell's strong emphasis on excellent customer service to individual customers went beyond formalities. It was more than an on-paper program. It touched everyone in the company. And, it led to impressive financial success. As a final comment on Sewell's approach to customers, it is instructive to consider both the title and subtitle of his book: *Customers for Life: How To Turn That One-time Buyer Into a Lifetime Customer.* Customers may receive superb customer service without establishing relationships with providers, but when customers freely elect to become "*lifetime customers,*" one can be sure that some important positive provider-customer *relationships* have emerged along the way.

CHAPTER 12

COMPANY CULTURE AND CUSTOMER SERVICE

A *coherent company culture* that stresses *Superior Customer Service* means a unifying theme is present in the thinking and behavior of each person in the company. There is not a lot of guess work. Most people within the middle leadership of a company know or can make pretty good guesses about how top management is likely to handle clearly defined customer service issues. Furthermore, most foot soldiers, the rank and file of a company with a coherent culture, will have pretty good ideas about how their top management will see fairly well-defined *customer service* issues. If the culture of the company is focused upon *Superior Customer Service,* one can be assured that the substrata of business behavior within the company will reveal an unending abundance of *positive customer service events.*

The reason these things are so is that communication, both intended and unintended, spreads rapidly through most company cultures. People tend not to be shocked or surprised by things that a company does because they understand the company culture. These generalizations hold true if a culture is positive and breeds optimism among everyone, or if a culture is egregious and spawns cynics in every nook and cranny.

No matter what the culture of a company is, it will influence *customer service.* If the culture is positive and supportive, each person will know it and will probably try to conform to what he thinks is expected of him. If the culture is negative, providers will not *stick their necks out* to try to give good customer service for fear that someone could say *What you did cost us money. It reduced our profits.*

Executive Leadership

In most companies, company culture begins with the highest executives. They set the tone for company culture, or, if they are new, they send the message that the current company culture will be maintained, or that the day has come for introducing a new company culture. The most important things about executive leadership are not the memos and directives these executives issue. What are most important are the things they do, the actions they take, and the examples they set for everyone else to follow.

Actions really do speak louder than words. If one fails to see outstanding examples of customer service in the leadership of a company, then one should start questioning whether or not the culture of that company is superior or exceptional. If a company strives to be known for a *Superior Customer Service* culture, the executive leadership must manifest *Superior Customer Service* in all that it says and does.

Albrecht (1992) pinpointed six skills that an effective service leader contributes to an organization. They fit nicely into the perception of what an executive does in helping establish an exceptional customer service culture: ***first***, he provides a vision and values, states a mission, and makes critical decisions; ***second***, he gives direction by identifying targets and goals; ***third***, he uses persuasion to keep the staff energized and focused; ***fourth***, he offers support by staying in touch and helping solve problems; ***fifth***, he stresses staff development by encouraging each person to do his best; and ***sixth***, he shows appreciation to keep things moving forward.

Philosophy and Values

The philosophy and values held by the leaders of a company help define the culture of the company. The philosophy and values of the leaders are reflected in the behaviors of the leaders; also, they are reflected in the ideas leaders share as they speak and write within the company, within clubs, civic groups, associations, and within surrounding communities.

Oral and written statements by the leadership of a company reveal both directly and indirectly the concepts, goals, and priorities of a company. Such statements illuminate the pathways along which the leaders hope to see the company march forward. Such statements reveal the long range vision leaders hold for company development. The leaders of a company should make explicit connections between the philosophy and values they embrace and the broad concepts they use to define *Superior Customer Service.*

Policy Statements

Policy statements are formalized opinions handed down by the leaders of a company. Their purpose is to give general guidance to the thinking and to the strategies that people should adopt in dealing with problems and challenges that are faced by the company. They grow out of the central values that are embraced by the company's leadership. In some ways, they may be seen as attempts to more fully define and extend the implications of the main philosophy and values of the company. Policy statements should include references to *Superior Customer Service.*

Standard Operating Procedures

The *Standard Operating Procedures (SOP)* of a company may be thought of as a set of day-by-day guidelines that help the staff of a company see concrete steps that can be taken to perform tasks in ways consistent with the company's overall value system. *SOP manuals should include direct references to the central concepts that define Superior Customer Service.*

Anecdotal Realities

Anecdotal realities observed and recited by the internal staff of a company and anecdotal realities observed and reported by outsiders having little or no vested interest in the company are the quintessential data that define the culture of a company. The phrase "*litmus test*" is often used pejoratively. In this context, it has a positive application. The "*litmus test*" for whether or not *Superior Customer Service* is woven into the culture of a company is a stream of anecdotal realities about *Superior Customer Service* that has been observed in the company.

If at the routine anecdotal level, as seen by people both on the inside and outside of the company, a company has become known as a place where *Superior Customer Service* is practiced and experienced firsthand by both *internal* and *external customers*, then that company probably has a *Superior Customer Service* company culture. Regardless of literature, brochures, reports, and presidential messages about *Superior Customer Service*, if *Superior Customer Service* is not routinely witnessed at the anecdotal level, chances are that it is not present and that it does not define a company's culture.

CHAPTER 13

CUSTOMER SERVICE TRAINING AND ASSESSMENT

If the leadership of a company is serious about elevating customer service across an entire company to the *Superior Customer Service* level, then it should accept the notion that *customer service training* needs to be an ongoing program. Training for customer service should not be *periodic training*, or *every-once-in-a-while training*, or *maybe-we-had-better-do-some-training* type training, or *it's-time-for-our-annual-training* type training. "*No.*" For a company that is committed to *Superior Customer Service*, *customer service training* becomes standard. It becomes normal. It becomes integral. It merges seamlessly into the fabric of the company. It helps define who the company is and what it is. Everyone in the company accepts it because they have been told and have come to understand that this is what the company is or what the company is in the process of becoming—a company known far and wide for *Superior Customer Service.*

Hand in hand with the notion of training for customer service is the idea of assessing the company's efforts to determine if its training programs are actually improving the customer service that it delivers. A company may believe passionately that training is good, but if objective methods for assessing the effects of training are not in place, how can one know what works and what does not work?

One of the best ways to understand the importance of assessing customer service training and performance is to look to the accounting discipline. Everyone understands the importance of regularly performed accounting functions to help business leaders be aware of those factors affecting the financial well-being of a company. One does not say with regard to accounting: *In a few months, I'll check to see how sales are going. In a few months, I'll see if the people who owe us money have paid us. In a few months, I'll ask accounting if we are making a profit or if we are losing money.* No, questions of these types are under constant review, at least monthly, typically weekly, and sometimes on a daily basis. Assessment of customer service needs similar attention.

Executive Commitment

Great forward movement by an entire company in the customer service arena is usually the result of strong executive commitment. When the executive leaders of a company articulate the vision of what can be done in this area and decide to commit to the massive long-term training effort to make *Superior Customer Service* the norm for their company, good things can happen. It is true that an individual employee, both highly dedicated and enlightened, can give *Superior Customer Service.* Such a person may be so focused upon giving *Superior Customer Service* that he or she is in a constant state of training-learning, ever seeking and searching for better ways of making the customer happy and adding value to his purchase. It is also true that such *Five Star Providers* of *Superior Customer Service* can help elevate the performance of others around them; however, individual *Five Star Providers* are unlikely to have company-wide impact. Sustained company-wide impact requires, most often, the visible, vocal, written, and exemplary support of the top leaders of a company.

Training Recipients

Some people think that those who really need customer service training are the front line people, the rank and file workers who interact with external customers on a daily basis. The higher one goes in the management hierarchy of any company, the easier it becomes to excuse one's self from things as pedestrian as training programs to improve his or her understanding of customers and his or her ability to interact with them.

After all, those of us in upper management are doing things that are ***really important*** *and that only we can do. Clearly, we must be doing things right—otherwise, how could we successfully maintain upper management positions? We can't take time for every training program that comes along. We are not experts in all areas. We cannot be expected to know how to operate machines, do accounting, fill orders, solve maintenance problems, or find solutions for IT problems, so why should we be expected to be experts in the customer service area?*

The problem with attitudes such as these is that they relegate customer service skills to narrow specialties that are performed by only a few people. The truth is that customer service skills have general applications. *Customer service skills cut horizontally and vertically across departments, divisions, and disciplines of entire companies.* They may have some highly specialized applications, but customer service skills are used by everyone in every location, division, department, and office. One doesn't need a unique position within a company to get better at relating to customers. ***Everyone*** can benefit from acquiring a deeper understanding and better set of skills for providing *Superior Customer Service.*

Each person in a company from the President and CEO on down to the first rung of entry level personnel needs training in how to understand customer service principles and how to apply customer service skills. If one occupies an entry level position that entails nearly zero contact with *external customers*, that person is still a customer service provider to his or her fellow *secondary customers* within the mother company. The better one serves fellow *secondary customers*, the greater the chances that he or she shall provide excellent customer service to *external customers* when such contact does occur.

One would not expect training programs for entry level workers, supervisors, salespeople, accountants, and the highest executives in a company to overlap completely. There would be some overlap and some specialization as well. What should be expected is that no one person is so smart, so skilled, so knowledgeable, and so far above everyone else in his or her understanding and practice of customer service skills that that person should be exempt from training. No matter how good one is, improvement is still possible and his or her skills need honing. Finally, if one is absolutely stellar in his ability to deliver customer service, then he or she needs to participate in training so that the *rank and file* that are around him or her may see firsthand just how good a person can become.

Responsibility for Customer Service Training

Prior to 1985 when Albrecht & Zemke (1985) published their landmark book titled *Service America!*, it was less common to see the concept of customer service explained in the broad terms used today. In earlier times, customer service was more likely to be described as a department in a store where repairs and refunds were handled than to be described as an activity that concerned or should concern everyone in a company.

With the increased attention that customer service has received, the many books that have been written on this topic, and putting forth of the argument that everyone in a company is involved or should be involved in attempting to provide good customer service, it should come as little surprise that the idea of a ***Chief Customer Officer (CCO)*** has emerged (e.g., Bliss, 2006). In fact, Goodman (2009) noted that "*... about one-third of major U.S. companies now have an executive with a title that implies ...*" he or she bears the types of responsibilities that would be borne by a CCO.

The CCO is a person who has peer status with the other senior officers of a company and is charged with helping define, develop, assess, and maintain the customer service emphasis of an entire company. Since this chapter is about training, it is natural to ask: *Who makes sure that training programs occur and that people attend them?* Well, that would be one of the responsibilities of the CCO. Additionally, the CCO would be involved in designing or selecting training programs, arranging for instructors, and seeing to it that training records in customer service skills are maintained.

The relative newness of this concept means that many of the ideas about the exact nature of the CCO's role, the extent of his or her authority, and the ways in which this person would interface with Presidents, CEO's, (Chief Executive Officer), COO's (Chief Operating Officer), and CFO's (Chief Financial Officer) are yet to evolve. Bliss (2006) discusses many of these issues in her book.

Following is a provisional definition of the CCO role that could be helpful to those wishing to establish such a position. For a given industry, the definition could be changed as needed.

*The duties and responsibilities of the **Chief Customer Officer (CCO)**, as seen within the context of preserving acceptable profit margins, shall include, but not be limited to, creating, implementing, overseeing, measuring, and maintaining policies, procedures, programs, and training that shall promote and establish **Superior Customer Service** as the ideal standard for business relationships among all internal employees, and between internal employees and all outside clients and customers.*

Certifying Customer Service Competency

Many training and consulting companies that are found by doing simple internet searches (e.g., by entering **customer service training** and **certification**) offer courses on how to improve one's skills in the customer service area. Also, many of these same companies offer certificates showing students have completed training programs, and, in some cases, passed examinations demonstrating some level of mastery of the subject matter.

It is nearly impossible to say how helpful such programs might be if one has had no direct experience with them, or, at the very least, carefully studied their training materials. To be fair, it would seem that any such program would probably offer some help whether or not the quality and quantity of the help received would meet a student's expectations. Although one would expect some high quality customer service training programs to exist, there is no widely recognized and commonly accepted training program in customer service that customer service experts agree is the "*gold standard*."

In the staffing industry, the *American Staffing Association* has established a training program and companion certification for *Certified Staffing Professionals* (CSP). At *Elwood Staffing*, all staff members who work in branch office settings are required to earn the CSP as a qualification for promotions and merit pay increases. As of 2013, approximately 80 percent of branch office personnel had attained the CSP designation. More *Elwood Staffing* employees have earned the CSP designation than have employees of any other U.S. based staffing company. In addition to helping staff to be better prepared to offer good customer service, it is felt that the CSP gives *Elwood* a marketing edge over competitors that do not stress the importance of the *Certified Staffing Professional* designation.

The training program that leads to the CSP designation does not at this time include an explicitly identified customer service module. Instead, the program focuses upon legal issues such as those embodied in the Family and Medical Leave Act (FMLA) the Americans with Disabilities Act (ADA), Equal Employment Opportunity Commission (EEOC) guidelines, and wage and hour laws. Also, the program covers various co-employment issues that are unique to the temporary staffing industry.

The kinds of information one is exposed to in the CSP training program and the skills acquired as a result of this training help the provider make appropriate decisions about the complex issues relating to today's contract and temporary workforce. The provider holding the CSP designation is assumed to be better equipped on average to get the job done to the satisfaction of the external customer than is the provider who has not received this specialized training and does not hold the CSP designation.

Turning attention back to *customer service training*, author Dave Elwood feels the field of temporary staffing should work toward a specific designation that would identify those providers who have mastered a minimum level of *customer service skills*. Such certification would not make everyone a customer service super star, but establishing such a program would be a step in the right direction.

There will always be those untrained gems of providers having such great natural talents and instincts to serve the customer that they will continually outshine other providers who have completed courses of study and hold certificates. However, development of formal customer service training programs with certification objectives is still a step in the right direction and the more this happens the better things will be for the entire customer service field.

Internal Customer Service Rating Systems

The best way for a temporary staffing business to assess the level or quality of its customer service would be to go straight to *primary customers* and seek their input and ratings. However, primary customers may not always be available and if they are available they may not want to take time to answer questions about how well their providers are doing their jobs. In fact, some *primary customers* have the attitude that providers should be smart enough to know about the quality of the service they are giving, good or bad, and if something is wrong they should fix the problem without having to bother customers in the process.

Another approach to assessing customer service is to look at customer service that is directed toward one's internal staff. Author Dave Elwood has argued and other authors have pointed out as well that the better the customer service among internal staff members, the greater the likelihood such treatment will transfer to the *primary customer*, the *external customer* (e.g., Rosenbluth & Peters, 2002; Mitchell, 2008).

This problem was tackled at Elwood Staffing by setting up a web based rating system. Once a week each staff person throughout the entire company made (***totally anonymous***) ratings of the quality of customer service he or she had observed that was provided by peers to 1) primary/external customers, 2) internal staff members, and 3) job applicants. The ratings were done on a five point scale in which 1 = unacceptable service, 2 = below average service, 3 = average service, 4 = above average service, and 5 = superior service. When a person accessed the program to make ratings, the people to be rated popped up in a spread sheet and ratings were done quickly by just clicking the mouse on the desired rating level, 1 through 5. The process took no more than a few minutes each week.

The design of the system was such that each person was asked to make numerical ratings for three to seven of his or her closest peers, subordinates, or supervisors. Also, a person could enter ***anonymous written notes*** about *any internal staff person* in any part of the company. Administrator of the program, author Elwood, could see both numerical ratings and comments made for each staff person, but could not see who made them. The anonymity feature of the program appeared to work as intended. Once a week, Elwood sent handwritten notes (anywhere from 4 to 14 notes per week), through the U.S. postal system, to each staff person about whom comments had been made. The essence of comments was shared. Sentiments expressed in the notes were always attributed to "third parties." It was Elwood's opinion that these personal notes received via the postal system were well appreciated. One staff member commented that she had retained "*all of the notes she had received*" from several prior years. This rating system was helpful and was a step in the right direction, but its highly customized design—program required modification each time a person joined or left the company—limited its usefulness. The system was discontinued after less than a year's use.

A web-based customer service rating system that applies only to corporate personnel is in use at Elwood Staffing at this time. All staff members are encouraged to rate (on a 10 point scale) the level of internal customer service provided by corporate personnel. Respondents are also able to submit comments to highlight particularly good or poor service. Participation is strongly encouraged but completely voluntary. The ratings and comments are shared anonymously with corporate departments on a monthly basis. At this time, the program is still too new and data are too limited for generalized conclusions to be made about the program's usefulness. The program could be expanded to cover more content areas and a larger number of internal employees. It is author Elwood's opinion that at some future point, regular *accounting* should be performed to say how well any company is performing in each *customer service* area, *external, internal,* and *associate* as appropriate.

CHAPTER 14

CUSTOMER SERVICE AND PROFITABILITY

The central theme of the *Two Factor Theory of Customer Service* is that high levels of customer service create high profits, or are associated with high profits. However, many empirical findings concerning *customer service* and profits are couched in terms of *customer satisfaction* and profits. Fortunately, the phrases *customer service* and *customer satisfaction* are closely allied from both usage and definitional perspectives. What this means is that research findings showing strong connections between *customer satisfaction and profits* may be interpreted as supporting strong connections between *customer service and profits.*

Shareholder Value

One way to assess customer service and profitability is to ask if customer service is related to stock prices of publicly traded companies. *If customer service is everything it is touted to be, could one expect high levels of* ***customer service****, as reflected in high levels of* ***customer satisfaction****, to be associated with high stock prices and lower levels of customer service to be associated with lower stock prices?* For an answer to this question, attention is now turned to a study reported by Chris Denove and James Power.

In their book *Satisfaction: How Every Great Company Listens to the Voice of the Customer*, Denove & Power (2006) of the consulting-research firm *J. D. Power and Associates* described an analysis of the relationship between customer satisfaction and shareholder values. Their summary finding was: "*... there is an intractable connection between high levels of customer satisfaction and increased shareholder value.*" When customer satisfaction was high, shareholder value was high. When customer satisfaction was low, shareholder value was also low. Claims such as these are music to the ears of people who advocate customer service, but they are persuasive only when they are supported by real data.

The authors hypothesized that increases in *customer satisfaction* scores were positively associated with increases in shareholder values of publicly traded companies. To test their hypothesis, they selected customer satisfaction studies they had done in 1999 and matched them with customer satisfaction studies they had done for the same companies five years later in 2004. They identified 29 separate companies for which satisfaction studies had been done in both years. Next, they ranked each company based on how its *customer satisfaction* score compared to its industry-type peers in 1999. Lastly, for 2004, they classified each company into one of three groups depending upon changes in its *customer satisfaction* ranking compared to other companies within its industry: *ranking improved, ranking unchanged, ranking declined.*

For example, if a company were in the injection molding business, they looked at the customer satisfaction rank of that company in 1999, as compared to other injection molding businesses, and then looked at their ranking again in 2004. If their customer satisfaction ranking in 2004 had improved by more than 10 percent of their peers, they were placed into the *ranking improved* group. If a company's customer satisfaction ranking had changed by less than 10 percent (either positive or negative) of their peers, they were placed into the *ranking unchanged* group, and if a company's ranking had decreased by more than 10 percent of their peers, they were placed into the *ranking declined* group.

The authors commented, "*What we discovered surpassed our most optimistic expectations.*" The median change in shareholder value for companies in the *ranking declined* group (companies whose customer satisfaction scores had gone down) was a 28 percent **decrease**; the median change in shareholder value for companies in the *ranking unchanged* group was a 21 percent **increase**; and the median change in shareholder value for companies in the *ranking improved* group (companies whose customer satisfaction scores had gone up) was a 52 percent **increase.**

Figure 14-1

Median Changes in Shareholder Values for Publicly Traded Companies: Based on Changes in Customer Satisfaction Rankings from 1999 to 2004*

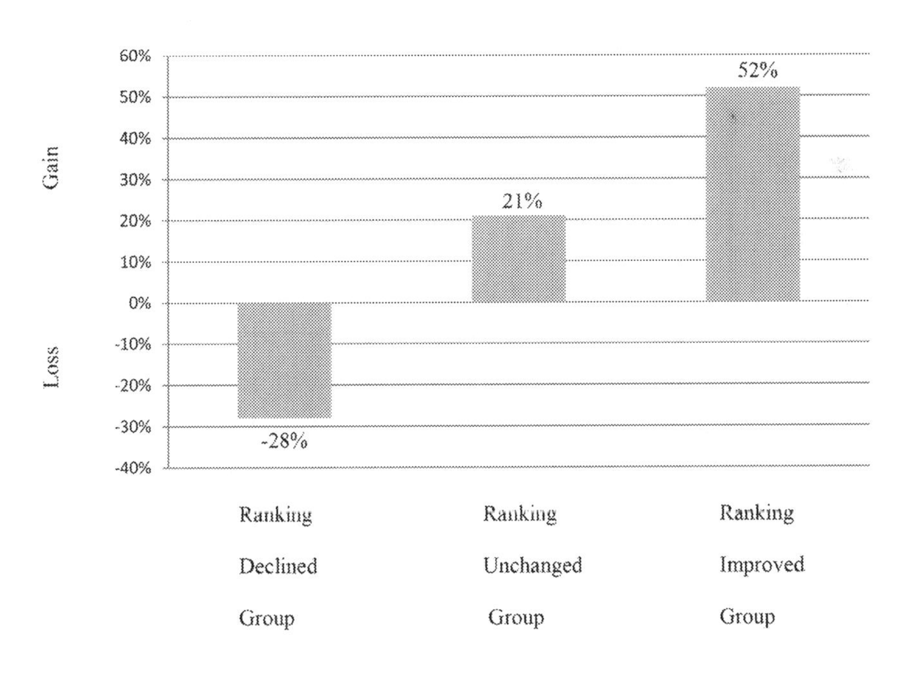

* Figure 14-1 was constructed using data provided by Denove & Power (2006, p. 5).

The results of this analysis shown in Figure 14-1 were that downward trends in customer satisfaction scores were associated with downward trends in shareholder values, and that upward trends in customer satisfaction scores were associated with upward trends in shareholder values.

Market Value Added (MVA)

In addition to stock prices, another way of measuring profitability is to look at *market value added* (MVA). Briefly defined, MVA means the difference between the invested capital of a company and its later market value. As an example, if one started a company by issuing 100 shares of stock for $1.00 per share, one would say the invested capital of the company at start up was $100. If after operating the company for one year things had gone so well that these same 100 shares of stock were now worth $10 a share, or a total of $1,000, one would say that the MVA was $900. The MVA was arrived at by subtracting the invested capital of $100 from the later market value of $1,000.

Claes Fornell (2007), author of the book *The Satisfied Customer: Winners and Losers in the Battle for Buyer Preference* and founder of the University of Michigan's *American Customer Satisfaction Index* (ACSI), presented data showing relationships between ACSI measures of customer satisfaction and MVA measures for publicly traded companies. If, indeed, high levels of customer satisfaction are associated with high levels of profitability, one would expect high ACSI scores to be connected with high measures of MVA.

Before discussing the data cited by Fornell, it is important to note four facts about the data. *First,* the data concerned average MVA's computed annually for publicly traded companies. *Second,* ACSI scores were available for all companies included in the data set. *Third*, the collected data covered a 13 year time span from 1994 through 2006. *Fourth*, for each year in this time span, two values were provided: *one*—the average MVA for *high satisfaction* companies (top 25% of ACSI scores); *two*—the average MVA for *low satisfaction* companies (bottom 25% of ACSI scores). Thus, for the 13 year time span, a total of 26 scores was provided allowing one to make year by year comparisons to see if MVA differences were present between companies that produced highly satisfied customers versus companies that produced poorly satisfied customers.

Here is a summary of what the data showed:

- for each one of the 13 years, average MVA's for companies with high satisfaction scores (top 25%) were greater than average MVA's for companies with low satisfaction scores (bottom 25%)
- the greatest difference in average MVA's for high satisfaction companies and was more than 12 times as much as average MVA's for low satisfaction companies
- the smallest difference between average MVA scores of high satisfaction companies was still more than 1.92 as great as the average score for low satisfaction companies.

All MVA data summed across years are presented in Figure 14-2. As a rule of thumb, the values shown in Figure 14-2 suggested that companies providing high levels of customer satisfaction (top quartile on ACSI measures) enjoyed approximately 3.6 times the MVA profitability as did companies providing low levels of customer satisfaction (bottom quartile on ACSI measures).

The summary implication of these findings was that a very strong and consistent association was present between ACSI customer satisfaction scores and MVA profitability measures. The consistency of the findings needs to be underscored. In ***each of the 13 consecutive years*** *for* *which data were provided, high satisfaction companies showed better profitability than low satisfaction companies. If one wished to make high profits, a good strategy would be to create as much satisfaction as possible by giving the very best customer service possible. Within practical limits, do everything possible to please the customer.*

Figure 14-2

Market Value Added (MVA) Averages for Publicly Traded Companies in Lowest and Highest Quartiles on Customer Satisfaction Measures for Thirteen Year Span from 1994 to 2006*

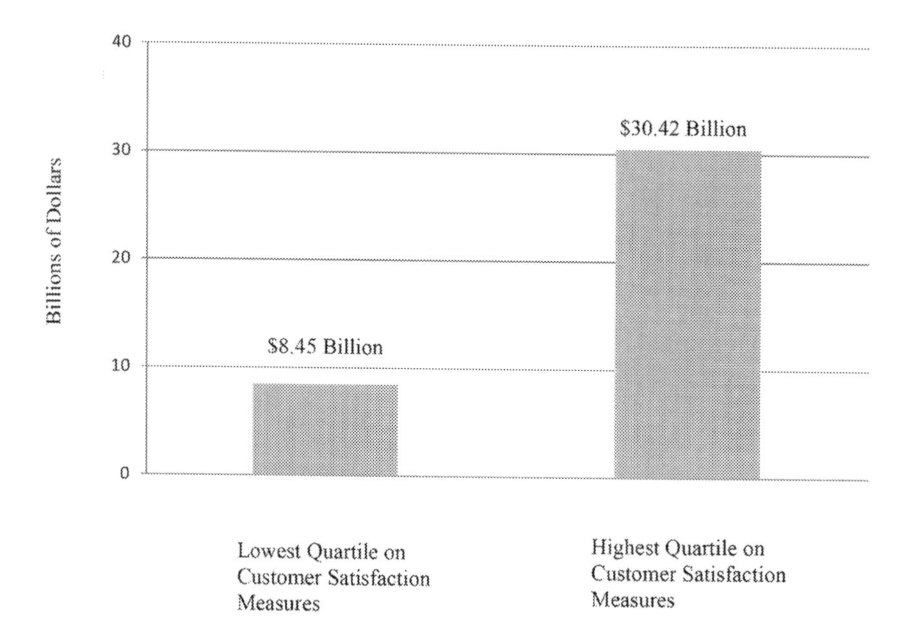

Employee Satisfaction and Employee Engagement

Empirical findings as reported by Denove & Power (2006) and Fornell (2007) were interpreted as supporting the idea that high

* Figure 14-2 was constructed using data cited by Fornell (2007, p. 206).

levels of *customer service* to *external customers,* thus creating high levels of *customer satisfaction,* were associated with high levels of profit and low levels of service to low levels of profit. *Since employees within one's own company represent a type of customer,* ***internal customer*** *or* ***secondary customer****, is it possible that satisfaction level of these customers could also be related to measures of profitability? If* ***internal customers*** *are highly satisfied, do profits go up; if they are dissatisfied, do profits go down?*

For help in answering these questions, one may look to the *Gallup Organization* that has generated a large body of research on *employee engagement. Employee engagement* and *employee satisfaction* are not identical concepts, but they do correlate highly which suggests they share characteristics in common. What this means is that high scores on measures of *employee engagement* were suggestive of workers who held high levels of *emotional satisfaction* toward their jobs and their companies, and, that low scores on employee engagement were suggestive of workers who were likely to be dissatisfied with their jobs and with the companies that employed them. *Where does this line of thinking lead one?* The answer is that if empirical data suggest connections between *employee engagement* and business outcomes associated with profitability, then one is probably also looking at data that support connections between *employee satisfaction* and profitability.

James Harter and colleagues (Harter, Schmidt, Killham, & Agrawal, 2009) reported a huge (the word *gigantic* would hardly be an overstatement) meta-analytical study sponsored by the *Gallup Organization* that focused on ***employee engagement***, was based upon 199 research reports, included 152 organizations and 44 industries, focused upon more than 32,000 business units within these organizations/companies, used data from answers given by more than 955,000 employees, and represented 26 countries.

The scope and depth of this study were enormous. The statistical techniques used were sophisticated. The conclusions drawn were powerful in the sense of being widely applicable. The conclusions were stable in the sense that refutation would be very improbable.

The authors studied the relationship between employee engagement at ***business unit levels*** (e.g., departments or divisions within a company; plants, stores, branch offices, hotels, or restaurants in different geographic locations; different schools or hospitals within a city) and nine business outcomes. Financial implications were significant for each business outcome. *What were the outcomes and what were the findings?*

Two major findings were reported. ***First***, employee engagement measures were significantly associated with all nine business outcomes. ***Second***, these associations were significant across all types of organizations. The results were highly generalized. What was true for one company, industry, location, and country was likely to be true for other companies, industries, locations, and countries.

The business outcome measures were:

1) customer loyalty
2) profitability
3) productivity
4) turnover
5) safety incidents
6) absenteeism
7) shrinkage (e.g., theft)
8) patient safety incidents
9) and quality

The implications of these findings were far reaching. When employees were highly engaged in their work, they were typically highly satisfied. The service they provided to outside customers appeared to lead outside/external customers toward greater loyalty toward their providers. Greater loyalty by the external customer implied lower costs to find new customers needed to replenish customer attrition. Loyalty also applied to internal employee/customers. When employees were engaged they tended to stick around for longer terms. They had lower turnover. They came to know their jobs better. They became more proficient in what they did. They had more opportunities to bond with outside customers. Less money was needed for recruitment, interviewing, and training to replace workers who had quit. When engagement was high, productivity tended to be high meaning one needed fewer people to get the same amount of work done. All of these outcomes translated into more ***profit***.

When employee engagement was high, workers were less prone to accidents. In the staffing industry, worker's compensation insurance is a significant expense item. Anything that can be done to reduce accidents is important. Fewer accidents mean lower insurance premiums. Highly engaged workers were less likely to have problems with absenteeism, are less likely to steal from their employers, and their work outputs were better quality, less likely to include defects.

Harter et al. (2009) pointed out that business units within a company (e.g., branch offices within a staffing company) that scored in the top half on composite measures of employment engagement had a 94 percent greater likelihood of scoring high on business outcome measures such as customer loyalty, profitability, and productivity than other business units within the same company (i.e., other branch offices) that scored in the lower half on measures of employee engagement. Furthermore, when comparisons were made between companies, it was found that those business units (be they stores, branch offices, hotels, restaurants, or plants) that scored in the top half on measures of employee engagement were 145 percent more likely to score high on business outcome measures such as customer loyalty, profitability, and productivity than were other business units scoring in the lower half on measures of employee engagement.

What it all amounted to was that workers who were highly engaged and highly satisfied appeared to contribute much more to the business success of their employers than other workers not engaged and not satisfied with their jobs and with their companies. As a concluding comment, the massive nature of the Harter et al. (2009; see also Harter, Schmidt, & Hayes, 2002) study made it exceedingly unlikely that another comparable study would be reported within the next several years that would substantially alter the main conclusion of this study: namely that, *compelling connections were present between employee engagement (and by implication employee satisfaction) and significant business outcomes that affected profitability. Give great customer service, enjoy great profits.*

Fortune 100 Best Places to Work

The *Fortune Magazine* list (published annually since 1998) of the top "*100 Best Places to Work*" in the U.S.A. singles out companies that provide extraordinarily positive regard, benefits, and opportunities to their employees. A company must have been in business for at least seven years and have no fewer than 1,000 internal employees to apply to be on the list. Inclusion on the list is based two-thirds on survey responses given by random samples of internal employees of a company and one-third on researchers' studies of the policies and practices of the company.

The giant internet search company *Google* was number one on the list in 2007. They provided five weeks of PTO (paid time off) after one year of employment. Sick leave was unlimited. The corporate office included 11 gourmet restaurants for the dining pleasure of its employees. Word had gotten around that *Google* was a great place to work—they received 1,300 resumes per day. A report issued in 2013 stated that the market value of *Google* had risen to over $325 billion making it the third most valuable company in the world.

SAS is the largest privately owned software company in the world. It has been on the *Fortune 100* list for 13 years and in 2010 came in at the number one spot. *SAS* provided high quality child care for its employees at $410 per month, paid 90% of health care costs, allowed unlimited sick leave, and maintained a staff of four doctors and 10 nurse practitioners at its corporate office to attend to the health needs of more than 4,000 employees on site. People at *SAS* were unafraid to say "*The customer is always right.*" And, they added "*Now you can be too.*"

Google and *SAS* are large companies. Can small companies qualify as great places to work since they lack the resources to provide perks such as gourmet dining rooms and fully staffed medical personnel to meet the health care needs of their employees? One answer to this question is that factors that influence employees' perceptions of the goodness of their companies as places to work are not always based on monetary or monetary related factors. The owner of a small company may, through the sheer force of his or her passion for excellence and sincere concern for the well being of his staff, create loyalty, motivation, and desire to provide *Superior Customer Service.*

One way to understand the "*100 Best Places to Work*" concept is to see it as recognition of high quality *customer service* directed toward one's fellow staff members who are, of course, *internal customers.* The executive leadership, a special class of *internal customers,* directs that all other employees give great customer service to each other. They all give great customer service and they all expect great customer service in return.

Now, the question must be asked: *Does having a great internal culture, being described as a great place to work, and, by implication, providing* ***good customer service*** *to both internal and external customers really make a difference so far as business success is concerned?*

Figure 14-3

Comparisons of Growth in
Revenue, Profit, and Market Value for
Fortune 100 Best Places to Work companies versus
Standard & Poor 500 Companies for Years 1998 – 2001*

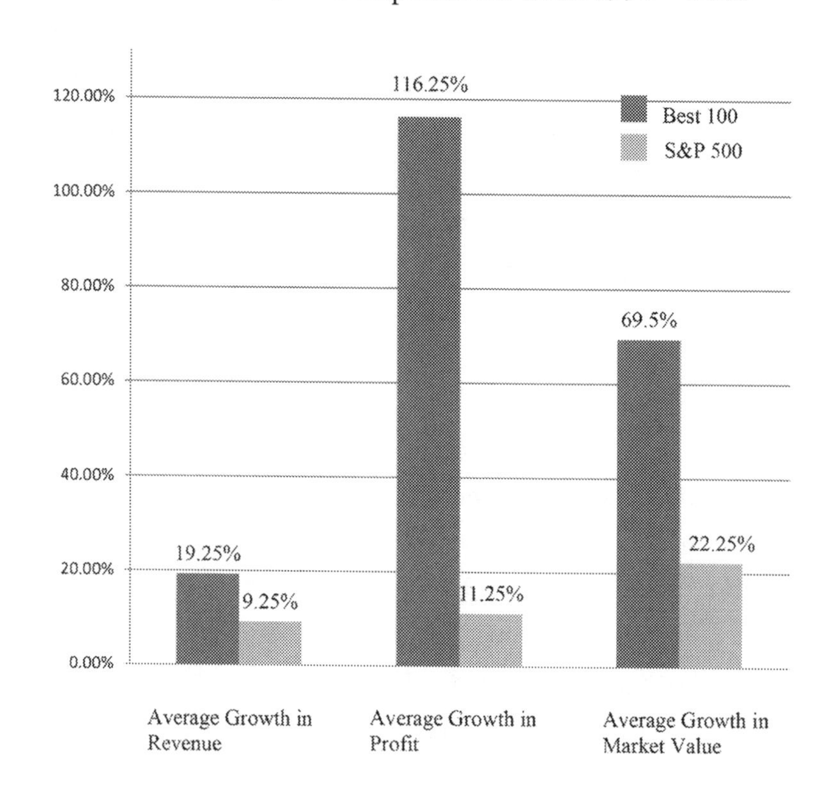

The answer to this question can be found in Figure 14-3. This figure was constructed using data presented by Heskett, Sasser, & Schlesinger (2003; p. 126) in their book *The Value Profit Chain: Treat Employees like Customers and Treat Customers like Employees.* Average data concerning percentages of growth in revenue, profit, and market

* Figure 14-3 was constructed using data cited by Heskett, Sasser, & Schlesinger (2006, p. 126).

value are shown for the *100 Best Companies* for years 1998-2001and for comparison groups of *S&P 500* companies for these same years.

What Figure 14-3 shows is that *Fortune 100 Best Places to Work Companies* dramatically outperformed *S&P 500* comparison companies. For the time period from 1998-2001, **Revenue** for the *100 Best Companies grew at more than twice the rate* of their *S&P 500* comparison group. Next, the figure shows that during the same 1998-2001 time frame **Profit** for the *100 Best Companies grew at more than 10 times as much* as for the *S&P 500* companies. Lastly, Figure 14-3 shows that **Market Value** for the *100 Best Companies* for this four year time frame *grew by more than three times as much* as for the *S&P 500* comparison companies.

The Service Profit Chain

"*The Service Profit Chain*" is an expression used by Heskett, Sasser, & Schlesinger (1997) to refer to relationships between measures of customer service, customer loyalty, employee satisfaction, profitability, and growth. A main implication of service profit chain thinking is that the better the customer service of a company, the more likely the company will prosper. The authors summarized the concept thus:

> "*Simply stated, **service profit chain** thinking maintains that there are direct and strong relationships between profit; growth; customer loyalty; customer satisfaction; the value of goods and services delivered to customers; and employee capability, satisfaction, loyalty, and productivity.*"

To illustrate their concept, Heskett et al. (1997) selected ten large well-known publicly traded companies (*e.g., Southwest Airlines, Wal-Mart, and American Express*) that showed evidence of management styles aligned with the service profit chain concept. Next, they selected ten large well-known publicly traded companies (*e.g., Kmart, Chase Manhattan Corp., and Coca-Cola*) that were described as "*reasonable matching comparisons*" (presumably, their management styles were less aligned with the service profit chain concept) for companies in the first group. Lastly, for the time period 1986-1995, the authors calculated indexes for growth in stock share prices for the a) service profit chain managed companies, b) for the "matched comparison firms," and c) for *S&P 500* common stocks.

The authors asked, "*What difference does service profit chain management make?*" Their answer: "*A lot.*" It was found that stock price increases for the service profit chain management group over the nine year span (1986-1995) was 147 percent which was nearly twice as fast as for the comparison group. The baseline group, the *S&P 500*, increased by only 110 percent. These findings plus the findings of Denove & Power (2006) and Fornell (2007) reviewed earlier in this Chapter all point in the same direction: stock prices are closely associated with customer-satisfaction/customer-service. When customer-satisfaction/customer-service increase, **stock prices tend to increase**. When customer-satisfaction/customer-service decrease, **stock prices tend to decrease**.

As a further example of how customer service qualities were associated with profitability, Heskett et al. (1997) described a study performed by the management of American Express Travel Services. It was found that when the 10 percent of ***most profitable*** travel service offices were compared to the 10 percent of ***least profitable*** travel service offices, the more profitable offices had been *rated by customers as having given more prompt and more accurate services.*

Southwest Airlines

Southwest Airlines has traditionally offered outstanding customer service. Heskett et al. (1997) presented data showing that for the period 1990 to 1995, *Southwest Airlines*, as compared to seven other major airlines such as *American, Delta,* and *United*, achieved the highest number of on-time arrivals, the lowest number of customer complaints per thousand passengers, and the fewest lost baggage claims per thousand passengers. One implication of these data was that stellar customer service was a reality at *Southwest Airlines*. But, the question must be asked: *Is evidence present that would suggest this seemingly great customer service was associated with or correlated with profitability?* The answer is "*Yes.*" "*The after-tax profits (at Southwest Airlines) in relation to revenues were by far the highest of any major U.S. airline in the five year period between 1990 and 1995*" (Heskett, et al., 1997; p. 24). Doing things promptly, treating passenger-customers so well that they rarely complain, and handling their luggage responsibly and efficiently were associated with earning the "*highest profits*" in the airline industry.

The evidence is clear that *external customers*, that is, passenger-customers, received good service at *Southwest*, but what about *internal customers* or *secondary customers*, the airline's own employees? How did they feel about *Southwest*? Apparently they felt pretty good. Heskett et al. (1997) reported that *Southwest* had been named one of "*ten best places to work in the U.S.A.*" and *Southwest* experienced "*the highest rate of employee retention in the airline industry.*" Lastly, note that the stock symbol for *Southwest Airline* is LUV—read as LOVE. It was selected to emphasize the great attention and care that *Southwest Airlines* directs toward customers—both external and internal.

CHAPTER 15

EXTRAORDINARY CUSTOMER SERVICE

For those having passion for the field of customer service, it is often inspirational to read accounts of extraordinary customer service. People like to hear stories about the lengths to which providers are willing to go to take care of customers and to keep them happy. If things are not going well and one feels frustrated, there's nothing like a fresh uplifting customer service story to get one back on track and refocused upon customer service ideals.

When extraordinary customer service is provided, what often happens is that in the normal course of business a customer presents a special need or problem. Then, an alert and caring provider leaps into action and goes beyond the call of duty to meet the customer's need and to solve his problem.

Providers should continually strive to deliver outstanding customer service, but common sense teaches that truly extraordinary customer service is not a daily occurrence. Can a rational standard be adopted so far as extraordinary customer service expectations are concerned? The answer is "*Yes*."

Two Factor Theory of Customer Service author Dave Elwood proposes that for companies fully committed to *Superior Customer Service*, it should be normal to see occasional reports of extraordinary customer service. If anecdotal accounts of highly outstanding customer service are not occasionally reported within one's company, it should be taken as a sign the company may not be committed to *Superior Customer Service* as its ideal.

Neiman Marcus

Stanley Marcus, the late legendary retailer of *Neiman Marcus* fame, said customers should be given all that they ask for without quibbling or debate. His opinion was that once a person starts debating with a customer, he loses the customer's good will. His attitude toward the customer was illustrated clearly in the first sentence of his book, Marcus (1974), *Minding the Store*, which reads "*There is never a good sale for Neiman Marcus unless it is a good buy for the customer.*" Whatever else happens during provider-customer encounters, it is important for the customer to leave the store feeling good.

During his early years with *Neiman Marcus*, starting in the late 1920's, Stanley Marcus balked at the idea of trying to keep the customer happy. He felt that a lady customer was at fault. She bought a $175 dress, took it home, wore it, clearly abused it, and then returned it to the store for refund. He argued this matter with his father, one of the founders of *Neiman Marcus* stores, pointing out that the store could not pass their loss back to the manufacturer.

His father listened patiently and replied, "*She's not doing business with the manufacturer, she's doing business with us. It costs us over $200 to get a new customer of this woman's buying potential and I'm not going to lose her for the $175 this dress cost us.*" He went ahead to advise his son, "*When you tell her (that you are giving her a refund), do it with a smile.*" The clincher for the story is what happened next. Over the ensuing years, this customer spent $500,000 in *Neiman Marcus* stores.

FedEx

Michael Basch (2002), author of *Customer Culture*, served as Senior Vice President of Sales & Customer Service for *FedEx* during its first 10 years of operation. He shared this dramatic story of extraordinary customer service.

As with many companies just trying to get started, *FedEx* went through some very trying times in its first months of operation. On January 2, 1973, 28 salespeople started working in 10 cities trying to sell the company's services: "*to deliver (a package) absolutely positively overnight.*" In addition to the sales people, there was a hub in Memphis, 23 airplanes, hundreds of other employees, and "*no money.*" The inaugural date for actually beginning shipment of packages was March 12, 1973, almost ten weeks after salespeople entered the field.

The salespeople estimated 3,000 packages would be shipped on the first night. Basch was skeptical and decided to probe more deeply. New estimate: only 300 packages would be shipped. Basch was in New York on the March 12 inaugural date for shipments to start, so he called the *FedEx* hub in Memphis to ask for a report about first day shipments. The manager in charge of shipping had good news and bad news. The good news was *six packages* had been shipped; Basch wondered what the bad news could be; the bad news was *four of the six packages* were sent by sales people just wanting to check the system. A few days later in the first week, *only one package* was shipped.

This less than stellar beginning for *FedEx* was disappointing. But, something good came from it. Many people in the company saw the urgency of their assignment: "GET THE PACKAGES." For example, some pilots would land their planes and then make sales calls. Other pilots would land their planes and then operate pickup and delivery stations. It was decided that if the company were to succeed they needed to serve a greater geographic area. They opened 15 new offices in 15 cities in 15 business days. By this time they were shipping 40 packages a day. It was a great improvement over day one but not enough to stay afloat.

One of the new offices was in Indiana. Two weeks after the office opened, a package "*tracer*" named Diane received a call from a lady in Indiana. She was in tears. She reported that her wedding dress had been shipped from Jacksonville, Florida and was supposed to arrive "*today*," but it was already 3:30 PM and it had not yet arrived. She was getting married the next day. Diane made six telephone calls and determined that the package was in Detroit, 300 miles away. She took the *FedEx* service standard, *to deliver absolutely positively overnight*, at face value. She took action. She arranged for an airplane, secured a pilot, and directed that the wedding dress be flown to the Indiana location.

The following Monday, Diane received a call from Mexico. It was from the Indiana bride wanting to express her great appreciation to Diane for making sure her wedding dress was delivered on time. Also, she asked to talk to the senior manager. The call was forwarded to Basch. After expressing her appreciation to him as well, she commented that it "*Wasn't all good news.*" She told a few people at the wedding about her wedding dress having had its own private airplane and thereafter the talk of the wedding was not about her. Instead, it was about this "*outrageous new airline delivery service.*"

The icing on the cake was that two *RCA* executives had attended the wedding and after going back to work, one of them contacted their traffic manager and made it clear that "*they should at least try*" the *FedEx* service. Thereafter, *FedEx* started picking up 20 packages per day from the *RCA* plant.

Basch reported that in the summer of 1973, a few months after the company started operating, the paychecks of 600 employees included a note reading "*Please don't cash the check because there's no money in the bank, but hang in there. We'll succeed together.*" Some would call it foolhardy that any employee under any condition should go along with a request such as this one. However, "*only a handful of people left.*"

One way to look at the response of those employees who stayed on was that it represented the deep commitment of one group of *secondary customers*, the rank and file workers of *FedEx*, to provide outstanding customer service to another group of *secondary customers*, the executive leadership of *FedEx*, who asked them to not cash their checks. The ultimate result was good. *After teetering on the brink of failure in 1973, sales for FedEx in 2013 were $44.3 billion with profits of $8.88 billion.*

Nordstrom

The *Nordstrom* department store chain enjoys an international reputation for great customer service. This reputation did not come about casually or recently. For almost 100 years, *Nordstrom* has emphasized "*Do what it takes to take care of the customer ...*" The leaders of the company encourage the public celebration of "*heroes*"—people who have gone to exceptional lengths to meet the needs of customers. The practice of identifying certain employees as *heroes* amounts to a methodology for transmitting and spreading the customer service culture of a company. The customer service focus of the company is further emphasized by empowering its associates to act like entrepreneurs and to use their reasonable judgment to solve problems and meet customers' needs.

Spector & McCarthy (2005) in their book *The Nordstrom Way* state that "*Nordstrom's return policy is virtually an unconditional money-back guarantee. ... If customers aren't completely satisfied with their purchase, for whatever reason, the store takes it back, no questions asked."*

The return policy is not empty rhetoric. In 2000, two Seattle women were packing some things to be moved when they ran across two pairs of forgotten never worn dress shoes in their original boxes along with a *Nordstrom* sales slip. When they returned the shoes to the store, the purchase price was fully reimbursed. The shoes had been bought in 1987, 13 years earlier.

The most famous story about the *Nordstrom* return policy concerns a set of automobile tires. *Nordstrom* has never sold automobile tires. But a salesperson "*gladly*" took back a set of tires and gave the customer a refund. Here is the background of the story as reported by Spector & McCarthy (2005).

"In 1975, Nordstrom acquired three stores in Alaska, from the Northern Commercial Company, which was a full-line department store that sold many products, including tires. After Nordstrom bought the stores, the company converted them to Nordstrom, eliminating many departments, including the tire department. So, when the customer —who purchased the tires from Northern Commercial Company (not Nordstrom)—brought them back to Nordstrom, the return was accepted."

Spector & McCarthy (2005) tell another story about the degree to which employees go to try to meet the needs of the customer. A customer in Seattle fell in love with a special pair of slacks that had just been placed on sale. The problem was that they were out of stock in the store where she traded. The salesperson called five other *Nordstrom* stores in the area to find the needed slacks, but she "struck out" at each store. She knew that a competitor across the street had the slacks, so she went over, bought the slacks at full price from the competitor, and returned to sell them at sales price to her customer.

One thing known for certain is that these types of stories about *Nordstrom's* customer service culture did not occur without a true and deep corporate commitment to put the customer first.

Staples

When one thinks of extraordinary customer service, he or she tends to imagine one or two anecdotal accounts that dramatically illustrate a company's dedication to satisfying its customers. But there is another way of looking at extraordinary service. Sometimes, what extraordinary customer service means is that someone had an idea for great customer service and was able to couple this idea with the energy and vision necessary to create a huge company while still preserving excellent customer service as the standard way of doing things.

The story of such a company is not so much one of anecdotal accounts of *Superior Customer Service* as it is one of a tsunami elevation of *Superior Customer Service* across a broad corporate horizon. For perspective, think of a company that started from scratch in 1986, emphasized great customer service from the start, was able to grow top line revenue to 24 million dollars in 27 years, and still maintained "*the personal touch.*" Most business owners would be proud of such an achievement. They would be keenly aware that the overwhelming majority of businesses do not attain such levels of success. But, this is the story of *Staples, Inc.* except for a minor correction—instead of growing top line revenue to 24 **million** dollars over 27 years, *Staples* grew top line revenue to 24 **billion** dollars over 24 years. During the journey, *Staples* went from one store in Brighton, Massachusetts to over 2,300 stores spread over 27 countries and became the world's largest office supply store.

Jim Peters, President of U.S. *Staples*, stated (Wiersema, 1998) "*We work hard to teach our people that great service is critical, and we empower our associates to take care of the customer at practically any cost." Is Staples still focused upon giving great customer service?*

Personal recommendation is the best recommendation of all. Author Dave Elwood stated that since there was no *Staples* store in the town where he lived, he often ordered over the telephone. When he called, a live person answered right away. He did not have to go through layer upon layer of automated messages before talking to a live person. The person who answered was always courteous, efficient, knowledgeable, patient, and helpful. He never had an unpleasant experience when talking to a *Staples*' representative. Orders were completed quickly and accurately and deliveries were made the next business day unless approved for later delivery for out of stock items. Even though *Staples* had become a huge company, they still had "*the personal touch.*"

A Man Named Fred

Mark Sanborn (2004), in his short, inspirational book *The Fred Factor*, told how the mailman who served his personal residence delivered outstanding customer service. The name of the mailman was Fred. Fred did not give outstanding customer service a few times, often times, or many times. He delivered outstanding customer service reliably, day in and day out, for over ten years.

Some things Fred did were to introduce himself to new customers, to present a cheerful attitude, to say "*Hello,*" and to welcome people to their new neighborhoods. He tried to learn something about new customers so that he could give them the very best service possible. For example, he asked customers to tell him when they would be gone on trips so that he could hold their mail for them. He knew that a stuffed mailbox could tip off a would-be house robber that no one was home. When Fred noticed that a package addressed to

Sanborn had been mistakenly delivered (by another delivery service) to a house several doors down the street, he retrieved it and brought it to the correct address.

Sanborn was so impressed by the outstanding service his mailman gave him that he started using his experiences with Fred as illustrations in speeches and seminars. He outlined four principles that he felt he learned from Fred the Postman.

Principle 1. *"Everyone makes a difference." "Whatever one's position or title, he or she can be an excellent employee. Nobody can prevent you from choosing to be exceptional."*

Principle 2. *"Success is built on relationships."* One can do a job impersonally, but it is better to do it within the context of a personalized relationship.

Principle 3. *"You must continually create value for others, and it doesn't have to cost a penny."* Fred created value for his customers on the basis of imagination and creativity—not on the basis of a budget to help him do his job better.

Principle 4. *"You can reinvent yourself regularly."* At times, all people feel limited motivation or that they are in a blind alley when it comes to increasing personal excellence. But, one is helped by considering what Fred the postman was able to do with *"putting mail in a box."*

When thinking of extraordinary customer service, one usually does not think of government organizations such as the postal service. Instead, one thinks of for profit businesses where great customer service is often dramatic and contributes to the financial success of the company. However, the lesson to be learned from Fred the Postman is that extraordinary customer service can occur anywhere.

CHAPTER 16

TIPS FOR DELIVERING SUPERIOR CUSTOMER SERVICE

Here are some basic ideas that can help each provider to more consistently offer *Superior Customer Service.* The ideas are practical and, if applied, will make positive differences in how people behave toward the customer.

Seeing the Customer's Point of View

Once in a while, one sees a provider who seems to hold, perhaps unknowingly, an attitude of *It's us against them.* Such providers seem motivated to hold the line, to make sure that no one gets by with anything, to enforce the rules, to keep customers honest, to make sure no one pulls anything over on them, and to search for customer infractions. All responsible business people want things to be done correctly and everyone knows that someone must "mind the store." At the end of the day, one needs to make a profit and if a business fails to do so, day after day, then eventually it will fail; it will cease to be. But, it is, nevertheless, unsettling to meet providers whose main idea of what *success-in- business* is all about boils down to a mainly *anti-customer* attitude. *Pro-customer* attitudes have a greater chance of producing true business success.

Providers should identify with customers. They should show genuine interest in how customers think and feel. Providers may be tempted to be annoyed with customers who fail to appreciate the *great deals* that providers give to them. But, it is usually counterproductive for a provider to criticize or scold a customer no matter how *paper-thin* the provider's profit margin. Providers need to figure out how to maintain positive, accepting attitudes toward customers. Some authors have attempted to capture these ideas in the titles of their books: Temporal & Trott (2001) *Romancing the Customer*; Miglani (2006) *Treat Your Customers*; Brinkman & Kirschner (2006) *Love Thy Customer*; Mitchell (2003) *Hug Your Customers*; and, Glanz (2007) *Care Packages for Your Customers.*

The main point these authors make is that positive relationships with customers are needed and that customers should see providers as friends, not as adversaries. One step that can help this happen is to teach service providers to work to see the customer's point of view and to be ready to do things to help the customer feel good. The customer needs to feel that the provider is his or her ally or advocate, not an adversary.

A story from author Dave Elwood's youth illustrates an attitude one should never have toward a customer. When Dave was a small lad five or six years of age, a brother Raymond (just two years older) and he entered a small neighborhood grocery store in their hometown of New Castle, Indiana. In those days, the 1930's, neighborhood grocery stores were quite common and a nickel was a lot of money. Raymond had a nickel which he placed into a Coke machine in eager anticipation of getting a cold drink. The mechanism worked fine allowing him to pull a six ounce glass bottle of Coke from the machine. In those days, all soft drinks, whatever the brand, came in glass bottles. While trying to open the Coke using the bottle opener attached to the side of the Coke machine, the entire neck of the bottle broke leaving a sharp jagged top making drinking from it impossible. When he showed it to the store owner hoping he would give him another Coke, the store owner commented: "*That's your tough luck.*"

That memory of poor customer service is still poignant to author Dave Elwood. Now, the store owner is long deceased, Raymond is deceased, the store has disappeared, and few people now alive would remember that such a store ever existed or what its name was, but Dave Elwood keenly remembers the store, the name of the store, its location on the northwest corner of the Main Street and "J" Avenue intersection, and the incident of poor customer service as though it happened yesterday.

Probably, each person reading these words can think of instances of poor customer service that he or she will never forget. Such memories may not go back so far as author Dave Elwood's and their recollections need not be matters of preoccupation, but the keen disappointment of bad customer service is easily refreshed and may affect one's willingness to do business with a company many years after a *poor customer service event* is long forgotten by the owners of a business.

Business people want customers to look back and remember how well they were treated when they entered a store and what great customer service they received. Those are the memories that lead to increases in contacts, inquiries, referrals, sales, and profits.

Finding New Ways to Please Customers

If one listens carefully to the customer, he or she will often make suggestions about how to give the best customer service. Sometimes, customers make suggestions in a positive, polite manner such as by saying "*I respectfully suggest that your customers would welcome such and such a change ...*" and sometimes their suggestions come in the form of angry complaints. How suggestions are presented, whether politely or rudely, is not nearly as important as whether or not one carefully scrutinizes all suggestions and complaints in search of implementable ideas that can actually improve customer service and—*increase profits.*

In addition to input received from customers, providers should be constantly reviewing, thinking about, and analyzing their own internal policies and business practices in search of improved ways of providing customer service. If one is innovative and creative, he or she could come up with ideas that could revolutionize an industry before customers or competitors ever dream of such new ways of doing things. But, most changes that one discovers about how to better serve the customer are not dramatic or revolutionary in nature. They are small, fine points that the attentive and perspicacious provider comes up with because he or she is constantly looking for, searching for, and uncovering that one small thing that will create an advantage over one's competitors. Remember that the difference between an Olympic medal winner and the person who gets no medal at all and whose name never appears in the record book may be only a few hundredths of a second.

Remembering Who Keeps You in Business

Sometimes, one gets so caught up in performing the routines of a job that he or she loses sight of what is important. Very few jobs are ends in themselves. They align with and attach to larger goals and objectives. In the world of business, the larger goals and objectives are customers and profits. The customer is what matters. Doing a job exceedingly well is important, but it is less important than making sure that whatever is done is focused toward and pleases the customer. In the words of Albrecht (1992), as shown in the title of his book, the customer is *The Only Thing That Matters.*

So, the goal, the focus, the purpose, and the obsession should be to stay in tune with what the customer is saying, thinking, feeling, and doing so that one may have the best chance of satisfying the customer, of meeting his or her wants and needs, and of anticipating what the customer will want next even before the customer has thought about it. The customer is the person who allows the owner to open his door for business.

Learning to Take Small Steps

There is a Chinese proverb that goes like this: *A thousand mile journey begins with the first step*. The lesson of this proverb is that if one wants to accomplish large things, he or she begins by accomplishing the small things that are the building blocks of larger things. That lesson is true for life in general and it is true for business.

Those who are passionate about customer service recognize that if one wants to do large things such as to establish a *Five Star Customer Service Program*, the way to start is by doing the small things that provide the foundation for such a program. One does not issue, on Monday morning, a purchase order for a *Five Star Customer Service Program* and expect it to be in place and humming along perfectly on Friday afternoon of the same week. To establish a mature program of customer service takes months and probably years because of so many thousands of little things that must be done by so many different people, in so many different situations, in so many different places, at so many different times, for such long times—then, and only then, does it become an everyday reality.

Although one must recognize, accept, and regularly perform the infinitely large number of small acts that define excellent customer service, a given way of providing service, even one that works very well, is not an end in itself. One should never get too caught up in or become too obsessed by any one of the individual building blocks of excellent customer service. Instead, one should be always looking toward doing things in better, more effective, more successful, and more satisfying ways that cause customers to continue to be pleased and delighted at how well they are served.

Making Each Provider Responsible

Many offices have break areas of some kind where one can have coffee, soft drinks, and snacks. In large offices where hundreds or thousands of workers are employed, there are full time staffs to serve food, drinks, clean tables, and keep things always picked up for everyone's pleasure and enjoyment.

In smaller offices which really constitute the majority of all business enterprises, everyone must help to keep the break area neat and clean. One of our staff put up this small sign (Text Box 16-1) in the Elwood Staffing corporate office to remind us that each person has a responsibility to help keep things neat and clean.

> Please clean up after yourself—washing all dishes and putting them away. Cleanliness is everyone's responsibility. There is NO "someone else" to do it for you. Thank you.

Text Box 16-1

The same thing is true in customer service. There is no someone else to give customer service. Everyone in the company is a customer service agent. All are customer service providers. The customer service burden is on the shoulders of each person. As one author put it so succinctly: There is no customer service department; you are the customer service department.

The customer does not care whom he or she meets with, what his role is, what his title is, or how much he is being paid. If there is a problem to be solved or a request to be fulfilled, the customer does not care who gets the work done so long as it is done, is done well, and is done promptly.

No matter what the business or industry, it may be that the single biggest challenge in establishing *Superior Customer Service* is to get each and every member of the staff to realize the depth and breadth of responsibility and corresponding opportunity he or she has to personally provide *Superior Customer Service.*

CHAPTER 17

THE MEANING OF IT ALL

The customer service culture of a company flows from its executive leadership. Such leadership is manifested in behavioral acts, written and spoken expressions of values, policy statements, and standard operating procedures. Cultural integrity means that all people from executive leaders to rank and file workers share and consistently practice the same understanding of customer service. Unscripted and unplanned *anecdotal realities* reveal the true nature of a company's customer service culture. If there is no stream of positive anecdotal realities, probably, *Superior Customer Service* does not exist.

Two Factor Theory of Customer Service

The *Two Factor Theory of Customer Service* represents a new way of describing and formalizing the relationship between a primary product, or range of products, and the customer service product. The *Two Factor Theory* states that the primary product and the customer service product go hand in hand. They are inextricably woven together. When one is present, the other is present. The customer service product is at rest behind the primary product until a sale occurs, then it springs into action and is thereafter present each and every time customers interact with providers.

A central implication of the *Two Factor Theory of Customer Service* is that companies do not have the option of providing or not providing the customer service product; even if it is ignored, it is still present helping or hindering the flow of business. If one is in business, he or she is in the customer service business. The customer service a company provides may be so lacking in quality that it contributes significantly to business failure. Or, it may be so outstanding that it helps maintain a business whose primary product is marginal.

Businesses, whether service, manufacturing, logistics, or professional are all formed to sell primary products that may be tangible or intangible. The primary product of a business is its reason for being, the reason it was able to open its doors on the first day of business. Customer service is an event, or a series of events, that are made possible and that depend upon the existence of a primary product. If there is no primary product, then, *ipso facto*, there is no customer service. The *Two Factor Theory of Customer Service* acknowledges and highlights the ubiquitous reality of customer service. It is everywhere; it is inescapable. Invited or not, it shows up.

Many business leaders fail to recognize that they have programs of customer service in place and have been paying for them ever since they started in business. Failure to pay attention to customer service neither obliterates nor renders it null and void. It continues to show up and to have effects even though it may not receive explicit attention, budget, or leadership.

The Customer

The customer is all important. One can have an award winning product, the best product ever made or offered, but without the customer to hear about it, understand it (in case it's an entirely intangible product), come and see it, touch it, feel it, smell it, taste it, eat it, try it on, drive it, ride it, fly it, or use it in some way, and, finally to buy it, then it does no one any good.

Because the customer is so important, crisp concepts are needed to tell who the customer is and to identify different types of customers. Sharp lines should be drawn between *customers* and *prospective customers*. The customer is someone who has bought something. The prospective customer is someone who may buy something. Five Star Salespeople have figured out how to discern between people in general and high quality prospective customers. High quality prospective customers are those who are most likely to become real customers.

The concepts *external customer* and *internal customer* have come into broad use and acceptance. These are helpful classifications. They remind people that fellow staff members who are *internal customers* play just as important a role in retaining 'old' *external customers* as salespeople play in acquiring 'new' *external customers*.

Author Dave Elwood has proposed that businesses adopt additional concepts to help describe those people who buy products and other people who influence the buying behaviors of those who make actual purchases. The concepts are *primary customer* and *secondary customer*. The primary customer is the person who pulls the trigger to buy. The primary customer is not a committee, a department, or a company. A primary customer is a person. The primary customer is the main person who finally says "*Yes*."

The *secondary customer* is the person who influences the primary customer. Always be courteous, polite, and respectful to the receptionist—she may be the best friend of the person who controls buying decisions for the entire company. They may have lunch together. They may be husband and wife! The boss may be very interested in any observation the receptionist would make about a salesperson, provider, or supplier. The receptionist is a *secondary customer*. The receptionist may influence the buying decisions of the primary customer.

The *secondary customer* concept also applies to the colleagues and fellow staff members of a salesperson. When a salesperson brings new business into a company, it is his or her fellow staff members who provide the main product and the customer service product to the customer. One's fellow staff members, by providing quality main products and good customer service products to *external customers*, or to *primary customers*, may influence primary customers to keep on and keep on submitting orders for main products. Indeed, one's colleagues are *secondary customers*—treat them well.

Everyone in the home company of the salesperson is a *secondary customer*. Each person "*back home*" in the provider company can have dramatic impact, good or bad, on the buying behavior of primary customers. In the staffing industry, it is easy to see how the *secondary customer* concept generalizes to the *temporary worker*, to the *associate*. *If the staffing company has a habit of sending* ***superb*** *temporary workers to a primary customer, will that not increase their chances of receiving more and more orders from that same primary customer?* Indeed, the answer is "*Yes*." And, indeed, is not the associate who performs so well on the job a *secondary customer*? The answer: "*Yes*."

Customer Service

Although many books have been written about customer service, there is no standard definition for customer service; here is a working definition.

Customer Service *is defined as the full range of interactions between a customer and any member of the provider company during which time the provider acted in ways that had positive or negative impacts upon the customer and the customer attributed this treatment to the provider or to the provider company.*

This definition is intended to be broad. Customer service permeates the entirety of interactions between customers and providers.

Customer service is a person-to-person activity, but it can encompass aspects of the physical environment if the customer attributes positive or negative sentiments about the environment to the provider. Well-designed main products are not customer service, although, they may make some aspects of customer service easier to deliver. For example, a well-designed automobile that works perfectly and rarely breaks down may lessen the chances that the service staff in an automobile dealership will have to deal with angry customers. Also, a perfectly functioning and highly reliable automobile could create such positive feelings that customers would overlook some customer service short comings.

Customer service starts the moment a 'looker' becomes a 'buyer.' Interactions between prospective customers and providers may be thought of as pre-customer service activities that are parts of the selling process. It is always important for providers to discriminate between customers and prospective customers and between customer service and pre-customer service. A wise and effective provider should be able to relate to prospective customers with such sensitivity that the typical prospective customer would be unable to detect a difference between the treatment that he or she receives and the treatment received by a *bona fide* customer. But, providers need to be keenly aware of the difference.

The location for customer service is anywhere and everywhere. Customer service may occur on the premises of the customer, on the premises of the provider, on the premises of both as in the case of telephone contact, or in a neutral location such as a restaurant, a meeting facility, or a grocery store where people just 'bump' into one and another. Regardless of the location and regardless of the reasons for meeting, if a customer and a provider interact and the customer goes away with positive or negative feelings or opinions about the provider, an incident of customer service has occurred.

Everyone in a provider company offers customer service. Those who are most visible are salespeople and staff members who deliver products to customers. But, any member of the staff of a provider company who happens to interact with a customer becomes a provider. The customer is largely indifferent to the power, rank, or influence of the provider who fills his or her order, solves a problem, or meets a need. The customer has his or her own problems to worry about and to solve. Customers want to present a problem or a need to a provider and then forget about it. They want to go ahead and deal with other issues that are critical to the success of their businesses.

Customer Service Events

Customer service events are those points of contact between providers and customers that result in customers attributing some level of sentiment, either good or bad, or some level of judgment, either good or bad, to the provider or to the company that the provider represents. Each time a provider and a customer interact, the event is pregnant with *customer service event* ***possibilities*** . However, a customer could feel neutral about most aspects of a contact. When this happens, a provider may have missed many opportunities "to score points" with the customer.

When providers and customers interact, one or more segments of the interaction must be *imbued* or *loaded* with some positive or negative sentiment or judgment, by the customer, in order for a *customer service event* to have occurred. The feelings and opinions of customers about providers and the things they do may be very mild or subtle and may not be articulated to the provider, but they are still *customer service events*. When customer service events occur, they are assessed, or measured, along the seven dimensions outlined in the *Two Factor Theory of Customer service*. The more skilled a provider becomes at assessing how a customer scores on these dimensions, the greater the likelihood that he can do something to improve his delivery of customer service.

Dimensions of Customer Service

Each dimension of customer service may be represented by multitudes of variables and measures. A given *customer service event* does not necessarily need to be measured on each dimension.

The ***Accessible*** dimension refers to a cluster of variables that all bear on how easy or how difficult it is for a customer to get into touch with a provider. To be accessible concerns street addresses, parking lots, office layouts, waiting room seating, number of telephone lines, number of people answering telephone lines, published telephone numbers, numbers of places where telephone numbers are published, days and hours when offices are open, person vs. automated telephone answering systems, signage, and internet presence.

Any condition that hampers, hinders, or blocks a customer or prospective customer's attempts to contact a provider is a condition that limits accessibility. Neither potential customers nor real customers want to wait, or to be frustrated, when trying to contact a provider. If the provider is attending an in-office meeting and a customer attempts to make contact, most of the time the provider should leave the meeting and accept a call from a primary customer. Few business activities are so important that they should take precedence over accepting calls from primary customers. *Real business* is more likely to occur between *providers* and *customers*—not between *providers* and *providers*.

The ***Temporal*** dimension concerns how quickly telephones are answered, how promptly one acknowledges a visitor, how soon one says "*Hello*" or smiles, how quickly a telephone call is returned, how quickly voice mail messages are returned, how quickly emails are answered, and, perhaps most important of all, how quickly an ordered product is delivered.

Temporal refers to how promptly responses are made, especially responses that are important to the customer. In general, quick responses suggest good customer service, and, in general, slow responses lean toward poor customer service. The opinion of the customer about what is quick and what is slow is usually more important than the opinion of the provider about what is quick and what is slow.

The ***Emotional*** dimension concerns feelings and emotions within customers that customers attribute to interactions with providers. Ideally, providers should always arouse feelings of delight in customers. Good emotions do not guarantee that all around good customer service has been delivered, but most certainly it is better for customers to go away feeling satisfied, accepted, appreciated, and happy than to go away feeling annoyed, resentful, or angry. Customers can overlook many aspects of poor customer service, but few will tolerate feeling emotionally mistreated.

The ***Informational*** dimension has to do with the range and depth of information that a provider possesses that can be used to serve the customer. Three types of information can be used by providers to serve customers: ***First*** is information about the wants, needs, hopes, desires, and frustrations or problems of the customer. ***Second*** is information about the product or range of products that providers and their companies offer to the customer. ***Third*** is information about the economic, legislative, business, and social environments in which business occurs.

The greater the amount of information possessed by a provider, the higher the level of customer service the provider can offer. In contrast, providers who know little about the customer, are uninformed about their own products, and know little about ambient conditions in which business occurs are ill-prepared to offer more than mediocre or poor customer service.

The ***Aptitudinal*** dimension refers to those aspects of behavior called abilities, skills, talents, and competencies that come from natural talent, training, experience, and interest patterns. A central implication of this dimension is that, on average, brighter, more capable providers can provide better customer service than their less capable counterparts. Whenever possible, select the brightest candidates to provide customer service. Also, select candidates whose vocational interest patterns are most aligned with the types of work they will be expected to perform.

The ***Solutional*** dimension of customer service refers to those aspects of provider-customer contact in which the customer has made a clear statement that he has a problem and that he is looking to the provider to deliver the solution. The customer may be upset about the problem or he may be quite calm. The problem may concern the primary product, the customer service product, or both the primary and customer service products. It does not matter. If both products are a part of the problem, both need attention. Even if a customer is quite relaxed about a problem he has brought to the provider, the provider needs to work quickly and effectively to fix the problem and to fully restore the customer's feelings, from dissatisfaction to satisfaction.

The ***Relational*** dimension refers to those patterns of spontaneous reactions, planned responses, and qualities of personality and character that help establish positive, enduring relationships between customers and providers. Behavioral qualities such as trust, respect, acceptance, and genuine interest in the other person, when manifested by the provider, facilitate establishment of stable, positive relationships between the provider and the customer. The high water mark for the relationship dimension would be development of a provider-customer friendship.

Customer Service and Profitability

Advocates for customer service claim that great customer service is closely related to high profits. Further, it is argued that significant budgets should be put into place to train all staff to provide *Superior Customer Service.* Arguments for customer service should be accompanied by objective data that support the argument that high levels of customer service are associated with high levels of profit. Data presented here show that customer service and profitability go hand in hand.

Several investigators have reported strong linkages or associations between *customer satisfaction* levels and stock prices (Denove & Power, 2006; Fornell, 2007; Heskett, Sasser, & Schlesinger, 1997). In general, the findings indicate that *increases* in customer satisfaction are associated with *increases* in stock prices while *decreases* in customer satisfaction are accompanied by *decreases* in stock prices. For example, Fornell reported that for year 2006, the average market value added (MVA) amount for publicly traded companies in the *lowest quartile* of the American Customer Satisfaction Index (ACSI) was only a *$12.1 billion gain* while the average MVA amount for publicly traded companies in the *highest quartile* of the ACSI was markedly greater—a gain of *$44.1 billion.*

Strong associations have also been reported between employee satisfaction (a measure of customer service that is directed toward one's own employees) and measures of significant business outcomes that include customer loyalty, profit, productivity, turnover, and safety (Harter, Schmidt, & Hayes (2002). If a department or division of a company includes highly satisfied employees, it is likely that they will be more productive, that their external customers will be more loyal, and profits will be higher than for other departments and divisions in the same company whose employees are less satisfied.

As employee satisfaction goes up, other significant business outcomes also go up.

Harter, Schmidt, Killham, & Agrawal (2009) reported a massive meta-analytical study based on responses from over 955,000 employees showing that *employee engagement* which is highly correlated with *employee satisfaction* was significantly related to these business outcome measures: *customer loyalty, profitability, productivity, turnover, employee-safety incidents, absenteeism, shrinkage (theft), patient-safety incidents,* and *quality*. The more engaged employees were, the better the business units in which they worked (e.g., stores, restaurants, hotels, department, and divisions) performed on the listed business outcome measures. It was notable that these relationships were true across different industries, departments, locations, and countries. The relationships were very highly generalized.

In summary, empirical research supports the idea that exceptional customer service is associated with high scores on important business outcome measures. From measures of productivity and safety to measures of absenteeism and theft, those business units such as stores, restaurants, and hotels whose employees were most engaged and most satisfied were the business units that scored highest on business outcomes measures that affect profitability. When all is said and done, **Superior Customer Service** should be a central tenet in the strategy of each company having a profit motive because empirical research shows it to be strongly correlated with business success.

Elwood Staffing and Superior Customer Service

In 1995, author Dave Elwood with an internal staff of two other people plus one half-time person, one office, no reserves in the bank, "zero" sales in staffing, no experience or know-how in staffing, and little to go on except a willingness to work hard and a resolve "*to try to figure out how to be successful in business*" entered the temporary staffing industry. At that time, the company was known as *Elwood Consulting* and its main product was pre-employment testing services.

Fast forward. Now in 2013, 18 years later, *Elwood Consulting* had evolved into *Elwood Staffing*, had an internal staff of 940, did business with around 6,000 customers annually, placed approximately 100,000 temporary workers annually, and was among the top 15 largest *industrial* staffing companies in the U.S.

By almost any commonly accepted standard, *Elwood Staffing* would have to be called a highly successful company. *To what does author Dave Elwood attribute the success of Elwood Staffing?* Before *Elwood Consulting* entered the temporary staffing field, there was a clear, consistent emphasis on approaching all business transactions with honesty and integrity. To operate ethically was a bedrock belief of the company. But, to strive toward high ethical ideals is rarely an adequate basis for business success. Hard work was emphasized and that too was commendable, but hard work, or hard work in combination with high ethical standards, do not assure business success. Another important element in the success of *Elwood Staffing* was perseverance. But perseverance, like hard work, and like ethical ideals, alone, or in combinations, do not assure business success on any great scale.

Two factors important in business success but not alluded to so far are a) commitment to finding high caliber business associates, and b) commitment to *Superior Customer Service.* Commitment to finding high caliber business associates had always had high priority. It was assumed that the most capable, brightest associates would get more accomplished and would deliver better *customer service* than would less brighter and less capable associates (Hunter & Hunter, 1984; Sewell & Brown, 2002). *Elwood Staffing* had always gone after the brightest people that could be found to fill high level leadership positions.

To round out the picture, as *Elwood Staffing* evolved into an increasingly successful and larger company, delivery of *Superior Customer Services* became a regular theme as a part of company philosophy, as a focus of training programs, as a guiding principle for service delivery, as a standard to be used by each employee in assessing his or her performance when relating to customers, and as an image of how *Elwood Staffing* wanted to be seen by customers and by the public at large. It is author Dave Elwood's opinion that a large part of the success of *Elwood Staffing* must be attributed to the company's unwavering commitment to routinely providing *Superior Customer Service* to all customers, both *external* and *internal.*

LIST OF REFERENCES

Albrecht, K. (1992). *The only thing that matters: Bringing the power of the customer into the center of your business.* New York, NY: HarperBusiness.

Albrecht, K. & Zemke, R. (2002). *Service America in the new economy.* New York, NY: McGraw-Hill.

Albrecht, S. (1994). *Service, service, service: A secret weapon for your growing business.* Holbrook, MA: Adams Media Corporation.

Bailey, K. & Leland, K. (2008). *Customer service in an instant: 60 ways to win customers and keep them coming back.* Franklin Lakes, NJ: Career Press.

Basch, M. D. (2002). *Customer culture: How FedEx and other great companies put the customer first every day.* Upper Saddle River, NJ: Prentice Hall.

Beemer, C. B. & Shook, R. L. (2009). *The customer rules: The 14 indispensable, irrefutable, and indisputable qualities of the greatest service companies in the world.* New York, NY: McGraw-Hill.

Bell, C. R. (1996). *Customers as partners: Building relationships that last.* San Francisco, CA: Berrett-Koehler.

Bell, C. R. & Bell, B. R. (2003). *Magnetic service: Secrets for creating passionately devoted customers.* San Francisco, CA: Berrett-Koehler.

Bergdahl, M. (2006). *The 10 rules of Sam Walton.* Hoboken, NJ: John Wiley & Sons.

Berry, L. L. (1995). *On great service: A framework for action.* New York, NY: The Free Press.

Blackshaw, P. (2008). *Satisfied customers tell three friends, angry customers tell 3,000: Running a business in today's consumer-driven world.* New York, NY: Doubleday.

Bliss, J. (2006). *Chief customer officer: Getting past lip service to passionate action.* San Francisco, CA: Jossey-Bass.

Bly, R. W. (1993). *Keeping clients satisfied: Make your service business more successful and profitable.* Englewood Cliffs, NJ: Prentice Hall.

Brinkman, R. & Kirschner, R. (2006). *Love thy customer: Creating delight, preventing dissatisfaction, and pleasing your hardest-to-please customers.* New York, NY: McGraw-Hill.

Carr, C. (1990). *Front-line customer service: 15 keys to customer satisfaction.* New York, NY: John Wiley & Sons.

Cooper, F. (2010). *The customer signs your pay check.* New York, NY: McGraw-Hill.

Denove, C. & Power IV, J. D. (2006). *Satisfaction: How every great company listens to the voice of the customer.* New York, NY: Portfolio.

Fornell, C. (2007). *The satisfied customer: Winners and losers in the battle for buyer preferences.* New York, NY: Palgrave MacMillan.

Glanz, B. A. (2007). *Care packages for your customers: An idea a week to enhance customer service.* New York, NY: McGraw-Hill.

Goodman, J. A. (2009). *Strategic customer service: Managing the customer experience to increase positive word of mouth, build loyalty, and maximize profits.* New York, NY: American Management Assn.

Harter, J. K., Schmidt, F. L., & Hayes, T. L. (2002). Business-unit level relationship between employee satisfaction, employee engagement, and business outcomes: A meta-analysis. *Journal of Applied Psychology*, 87, 268-279.

Harter, J. K., Schmidt, F. L., Killham, E. A., & Agrawal, S. (2009). *Q12 Meta-Analysis: The relationship between engagement at work and organizational outcomes.* Washington, D.C.: Gallup University Press.

Heskett, J. L., Sasser, Jr., W. E., & Schlesinger, L. A. (1997). *The service profit chain: How leading companies link profit and growth through loyalty, satisfaction, and value.* New York, NY: The Free Press.

Heskett, J. L., Sasser, Jr., W. E., & Schlesinger, L. A. (2003). *The value profit chain: Treat employees like customers and customers like employees.* New York, NY: The Free Press.

Holland, J. E. (1994). *SDS: Self-Directed Search, Form R, 4th Edition.* Lutz, FL: Psychological Assessment Resources.

Holland, J. E., Fritzsche, B. A., & Powell, A. B. (1997). *SDS: Self-Directed Search Technical Manual.* Lutz, FL: Psychological Assessment Resources.

Hunter, J. E. & Hunter, R. F. (1984). Validity and utility of alternative predictors of job performance. *Psychological Bulletin*, 96, 72-98.

Hyken, S. (2009). *The cult of the customer: Create an amazing customer experience that turns satisfied customers into customer evangelists.* Hoboken, NJ: John Wiley & Sons.

Kaufman, R. (2012). *Uplifting service: The proven path to delighting your customers, colleagues, and everyone else you meet.* New York, NY: Evolve Publishing.

Kazanjian, K. (2007). *Exceeding customer expectations: What Enterprise, America's #1 car rental company, can teach you about creating lifetime customers.* New York, NY: Doubleday.

Kuratko, D. F. (2009). *Entrepreneurship: Theory, process, practice: Eighth edition.* Mason, OH: South-Western Cengage Learning.

Lawfer, M. R. (2004). *Why customers come back: How to create lasting customer loyalty.* Franklin Lakes, NJ: Career Press.

LeBoeuf, M. (2000). *How to win customers and keep them for life, revised.* New York, NY: Berkley Books.

Lewin, K. (1945). The research center for group dynamics at the Massachusetts Institute for Technology. *Sociometry*, 8, 126-135.

Livingston, A. (Ed). (June 2008). *The condition of education 2008 in brief.* U.S. Department of Education: Institute for Education Science, NCES 2008-032.

Marcus, S. (1974). *Minding the store.* New York, NY: The New American Library.

Massnick, F. (1997). *The customer is CEO: How to measure what your customers want—and make sure they get it.* New York, NY: American Management Assn.

Miglani, B. (2006). *Treat your customers: Thirty lessons on service that I learned at my family's Dairy Queen store.* New York, NY: Hyperion.

Mitchell, J. (2008). *Hug your customers: The proven way to personalize sales and achieve astounding results.* New York, NY: Hyperion.

Peters, T. (1994). *The pursuit of wow!: Every person's guide to topsy-turvy times.* New York, NY: Random House.

Rosenbluth, H. F. & Peters, D. M. (2002). *The customer comes second: Put your people first and watch'em kick butt.* New York, NY: HarperCollins.

Sanborn, M. (2004). *The Fred factor: How passion in your work and life can turn the ordinary into the extraordinary.* Colorado Springs, CO: Waterbrook Press.

Schmidt, F. L. & Hunter, J. E. (1998). The validity and utility of selection methods in personnel psychology: Practical and theoretical implications of 85 years of research findings. *Psychological Bulletin*, 124, 262-274.

Schmitt, B. H. (2003). *Customer experience management: A revolutionary approach to connecting with your customers.* New York, NY: John Wiley & Sons.

Sewell, C. & Brown, P. B. (2002). *Customers for life: How to turn that one-time buyer into a lifetime customer.* New York, NY: Doubleday.

Snow, D. & Yanovitch, T. (2003). *Unleashing excellence: The complete guide to ultimate customer service.* Sanford, FL: DC Press.

Spector, R. & McCarthy, P. (2005). *The Nordstrom way to customer service excellence: A handbook for implementing great service in your organization.* Hoboken, NJ: John Wiley & Sons.

Temporal, P. & Trott, M. (2001). *Romancing the customer: Maximizing brand value through powerful relationship management.* New York, NY: John Wiley & Sons.

Timm, P. R. (2001). *Seven power strategies for building customer loyalty.* New York, NY: American Management Assn.

Whiteley, R. C. (1991). *The customer-driven company: Moving from talk to action.* Reading, MA: Addison-Wesley.

Whiteley, R. & Hessan, D. (1996). *Customer centered growth: Five proven strategies for building competitive advantage.* Reading, MA: Addison-Wesley.

Wiersema, F. (Ed.). (1998). *Customer service: Extraordinary results at Southwest Airlines, Charles Schwab, Lands' End, American Express, Staples, and USAA.* New York, NY: HarperBusiness.

Willingham, R. (1992). *Hey, I'm the customer.* Paramus, NJ: Prentice Hall.

Zeithaml, V. A., Parasuraman, A., & Berry, L. L. (1990). *Delivering quality service: Balancing customer perceptions and expectations.* New York, NY: The Free Press.

INDEX

B

C

D

E

F

G

H

I

J & K

L

Q & R

S

T

U & V

W

X, Y & Z

Printed in the United States
By Bookmasters